2nd Workshop on the Creative AI Meets Conversational AI (CAI2)

Held at COLING 2022

Gyeongju, South Korea
12 – 17 October 2022

ISBN: 978-1-7138-6146-1

Printed from e-media with permission by:

Curran Associates, Inc.
57 Morehouse Lane
Red Hook, NY 12571

Some format issues inherent in the e-media version may also appear in this print version.

Association for Computational Linguistics
209 N. Eighth Street
Stroudsburg, Pennsylvania 18360

Phone: 1-570-476-8006
Fax: 1-570-476-0860

acl@aclweb.org

Additional copies of this publication are available from:

Curran Associates, Inc.
57 Morehouse Lane
Red Hook, NY 12571 USA
Phone: 845-758-0400
Fax: 845-758-2633
Email: curran@proceedings.com
Web: www.proceedings.com

CAI2

The Second Workshop on When Creative AI Meets Conversational AI

Proceedings of the Workshop

CAI2

Volume 29 (2022), No. 1

Proceedings of the Workshop

The 2nd Workshop on When Creative AI Meets Conversational AI

October 12 - 17, 2022
Gyeongju, Republic of Korea (Online)

ISSN 2951-2093

Introduction

It is our great pleasure to welcome you to the Second Workshop on When Creative AI Meets Conversational AI (CAI2).

This workshop focuses on intersection directions of creative AI and conversational AI that are influencing millions of people by real-world applications, such as digital assistants, virtual singers, voice boxes and metaverse. With the rapid development of emotional, creative digital assistants, we believe that future conversational AI systems can be further enhanced and boosted by the rapid developing creative AI technique: poeming, painting, gaming, and singing.

We have received a large number of submissions and accepted 9 long and short research papers. The papers cover directions of emotional chatbots, task-oriented question answering, humor detection, language models for speech recognition, task-oriented data construction, AI writing assisting, dialog controlling by prompts, food preference detection through conversation, and diffusion models for artwork creation.

We would like to thank everyone who submitted a paper to the workshop. We would also like to express our gratitude to the members of the Program Committee for their timely reviews, and for supporting the tight schedule by providing reviews at short notice.

We hope that you enjoy the workshop!

The CAI2 Organizers

October 2022

Organizing Committee

Xianchao Wu (He, NVIDIA)

Gang Niu (He, RIKEN)

Lin Gu (He, RIKEN)

Peiying Ruan (She, NVIDIA)

Haitao Yu (He, University of Tsukuba)

Xuemeng (Maggie) Zhang (She, NVIDIA)

Yi Dong (He, NVIDIA)

Hao Gong (He, NVIDIA)

PC Members

Yi Zhao (She, Kwai)

Yulan Yan (She, Databricks)

Sheng Li (He, NICT)

Chunmeng Ma (He, Fujitsu)

Table of Contents

Prompting for a conversation: How to control a dialog model?

Josef Valvoda[*] **Yimai Fang** **David Vandyke**
University of Cambridge Apple
jv406@cam.ac.uk
{yimai_fang,dvandyke}@apple.com

Abstract

Dialog modelling faces a difficult trade-off. Models are trained on a large amount of text, yet their responses need to be limited to a desired scope and style of a dialog agent. Because the datasets used to achieve the former contain language that is not compatible with the latter, pre-trained dialog models are fine-tuned on smaller curated datasets. However, the fine-tuning process robs them of the ability to produce diverse responses, eventually reducing them to *dull* conversation partners. In this paper we investigate if prompting can mitigate the above trade-off. Specifically, we experiment with conditioning the prompt on the query, rather than training a single prompt for all queries. By following the intuition that freezing the pre-trained language model will conserve its expressivity, we find that compared to fine-tuning, prompting can achieve a higher BLEU score and substantially improve the diversity and novelty of the responses.

1 Introduction

Prompting large language models (LLM) has recently demonstrated an impressive performance on a number of natural language processing (NLP) tasks such as machine translation (Radford et al., 2019), summarisation (Li and Liang, 2021) or question answering (Schick and Schütze, 2021a). Prompts are tokens which are appended or prepended to the input of a language model. They are employed to induce the model into generating useful information, while keeping the model weights frozen. Soft prompts, continuous trainable vectors prepended to the model input, have in particular proven useful for a number of tasks (Liu et al., 2021a). While requiring fine-tuning of only a relatively small number of parameters, they excel in a few-shot setting. Furthermore, as the underlying LLM's grow in parameter size, they become competitive even in the full data setting (Lester et al., 2021). Simultaneously, prompts remove the burden of storing the full copy of a fine-tuned LLM for every task, which becomes increasingly useful as the LLM size grows. Crucially for us, prompting preserves the LLM parameters which should help retain their general language abilities for a downstream task.

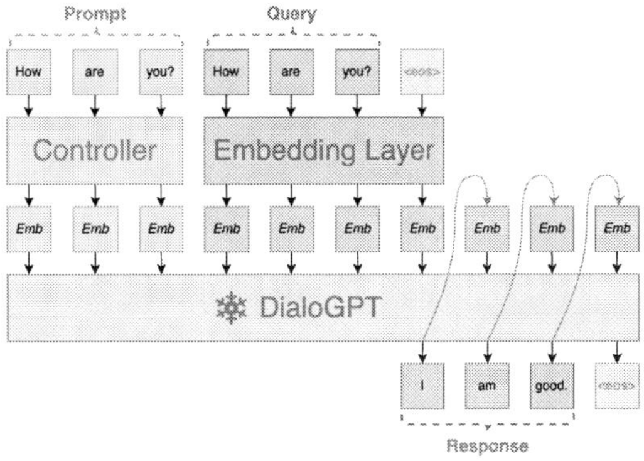

Figure 1: Dynamic prompt conditions the *prompt* on the *query* using the *controller*; a Transformer encoder.

Dialog modelling is the task of generating a response given the previous dialog turn, the query (Li et al., 2016b). Dialog models are typically trained using the maximum-likelihood estimation (MLE) objective. However, MLE-trained models have a high propensity to provide dull responses, such as *"I don't know"* (Sordoni et al., 2015; Serban et al., 2016; Zhao et al., 2017). While state-of-the-art models, such as DialoGPT (Zhang et al., 2020), can overcome this issue by training large models on massive amounts of data, a trade-off emerges. On the one hand, these models are expressive by virtue of the large datasets they are trained on. On the other hand, the same scale of training data and model parameters is responsible for the lack of control over the content of their responses.

Since dialog models are not useful without the ability to control their responses, in this paper, we

[*] Work done while at Apple.

Proceedings of the 2nd Workshop on When Creative AI Meets Conversational AI (CAI2), COLING 2022, pages 1–8
October 12–17, 2022.

turn to prompting as a possible method of exerting such control. Instead of fine-tuning the entire model, we keep the weights of the model intact, tuning only the prompts (and word embeddings) in an effort to preserve the models' expressivity. Furthermore, we develop a **dynamic-prompt**,[1] which conditions the prompt on the query in an effort to dynamically induce the response by having a different prompt for every turn of the conversation, see Fig. 1. The intuition is to separate the task of language generation, which LLM's are very good at, from the task of selecting appropriate responses, which LLM's struggle to learn from the limited examples they are fine-tuned on.

In our experiments with DailyDialog dataset, we find that the dynamic prompt outperforms both fine-tuning and the soft-prompting of DialoGPT in terms of a BLEU4 score. The best dynamic prompt model achieves 0.12 BLEU4 compared to 0.11 and 0.08 of fine-tuning and soft-prompting respectively. Furthermore, the dynamic prompt finds the best trade-off between the BLEU score and novelty as well as the diversity of responses, maintaining above 0.90 novelty and diversity as the BLEU4 score increases, while the other models can not. Finally, we find that dynamic-prompting on GPT-2 achieves the best BLEU4 results, improving over prompted DialoGPT by an additional 19% and casting doubt about the utility of dialog-specific pre-training when it comes to prompting.

2 Prompting for Dialog Generation

Fine-tuning a pre-trained model on a small dialog dataset degrades the novelty of the responses (Sordoni et al., 2015). Prompting opens up a possibility of exerting control over the model behaviour, without touching the majority of the weights that might be useful for generating novel responses (Lester et al., 2021). However, typical prompting methods are restrained in using a single prompt for a single task. In this section, we motivate the dynamic prompt as a natural next step in generalising the prompting paradigm for dialog modelling.

Prompting. Auto-regressive models with billions of parameters trained on a language modelling objective, such as OpenAI's GPT-3 (Brown et al., 2020), have demonstrated a strong few-shot performance without the need to update the model parameters. Instead of fine-tuning the model with target task examples, a manually designed prompt, for example in the form of a natural language sentence describing the task, is fed to the model to solicit the desired response. For instance, to induce a translation the model might be told to: *Translate English to French*. The description is followed up with pairs of examples of English sentences and their French translations. To derive a new translation the model is fed an English sentence alone and it is left to infer the French translation. However, not all human-designed prompts elicit the desired response. In practice ensembles of many prompts have gone some way in improving the performance, but still necessitate humans in the loop to design the said prompts (Schick and Schütze, 2021a).

Soft-prompting. To address this short-coming, recent work has found that prefixing and fine-tuning vocabulary tokens is a more expressive solution, which can learn the prompt from the data directly, without a need of a human prompt designer (Liu et al., 2021a). The soft prompts are not constrained by encoding existing tokens in the vocabulary and can freely encode parameters to facilitate the task. Empirically, soft prompts achieve better performance than their *hard* prompt counterparts and in a few-shot setting outperform fine-tuning of the entire model.

Dynamic-prompting. Soft prompts are restricted in utilising only a single prompt of a constant number of tokens for each task. We hypothesise that there are many tasks where the desired response for every input will be hard to solicit through a single shared general prompt. For example, the task of dialog generation has a general requirement to generate semantically and syntactically coherent, engaging responses. However, an individual response might have specific properties that are only relevant within the context of the query. While soft prompts are likely to solicit the more general tasks, such as machine translation or question answering, possibly because they exist in the training data to begin with, the more nuanced requirements might be heavily context-dependent. Therefore,

[1]Our work is concurrent to Gu et al. (2021) who develop a similar prompting method. However, our research is motivated by a different question from theirs. Specifically, we investigate how prompting can help with inducing creative responses, which we measure on the novelty and diversity metrics introduced below. Their work, on the other hand, focuses on improving performance on traditional metrics such as BLEU, NIST, METEOR and ROUGE-L.

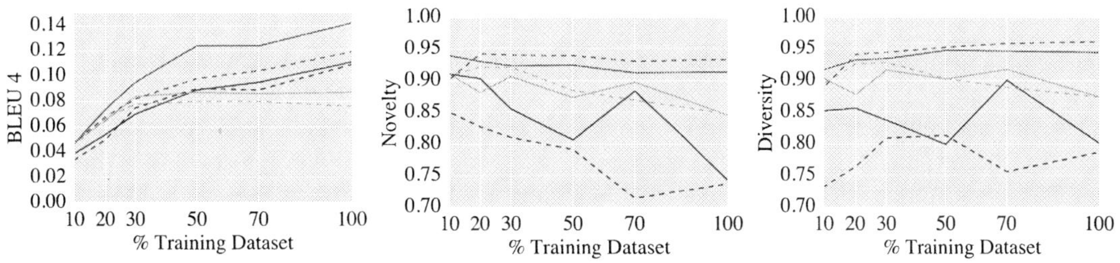

Figure 2: BLEU4, novelty and diversity scores for **fine-tuning**, **soft-prompting** and **dynamic-prompting**. Full line is GPT-2, dashed line is DialoGPT.

we condition the prompt on the context to enable learning different prompts for different queries. We describe the method in detail below.

3 Method

Notation. Let a dialogue be denoted as $x_1 \cdots x_N$ where N is the sequence length. We denote dialogue history as $S = x_1, \cdots, x_m$ and target sequence as $T = x_{m+1}, \cdots, x_N$. Now we can compute the conditional probability $P(T \mid S)$ as a product of a series of conditional probabilities:

$$p(T \mid S) = \prod_{n=m+1}^{N} p\left(x_n \mid x_1, \cdots, x_{n-1}\right) \quad (1)$$

This probability can be parametrized by an autoregressive language model (in our case DialoGPT).

Fine-tuning. For our experimental baseline, we simply fine-tune pre-trained DialoGPT on the DailyDialog dataset, see § 4.

Soft-prompting. For soft-prompting, we prepend a prompt $F = z_1, \cdots, z_m$ at the beginning of S. Prompt tokens are randomly initialised word embeddings appended to the DialoGPT vocabulary. In our experiments, we set the length of the soft prompt to the length of S. Now, to compute the probability of the target given the dialogue history and prompt, we compute:

$$p(T \mid S, F) = \prod_{n=m+1}^{N} p\left(x_n \mid z_1, \cdots, z_m, x_1, \cdots, x_{n-1}\right) \quad (2)$$

We instantiate the pre-trained DiaoGPT, but this time we freeze all of the model parameters, except the word embedding weights. While in a typical soft-prompting experiment only the prompt embeddings are tuned, we found that for our dialog setting the performance suffers considerably when the model is constrained to train only the parameters of prompt embeddings, which is why we relax this requirement. Furthermore, we do not calculate the loss for the logits corresponding to the prompt. This is because we don't know the ground truth of what the prompt should be.

Dynamic-prompting. Finally, we extend the soft-prompting paradigm by conditioning the prompt F on the query S to find a unique prompt for every query, see Fig. 1. We use an autoregressive Transformer encoder to generate the prompt embeddings:

$$\mathbf{h}_1, \cdots, \mathbf{h}_m = \mathrm{Transformer}(x_1, \cdots, x_m) \quad (3)$$

Now, we use $\mathbf{h}$ as our prompt token embeddings and prepend them to the query embeddings inside the DialoGPT model. The model is otherwise trained the same way as the soft-prompting model above. The Transformer encoder is trained jointly with the embeddings.

4 Experimental Setup

Datasets. We conduct our experiments on the DailyDialog dataset consisting of $13,118$ dialogues, split into $11,118$/$1,000$/$1,000$ training/validation/test sets (Li et al., 2017). We only focus on single-turn dialog modelling and process the dataset so that our pairs of queries and responses correspond to every two steps in a conversation. Inspired by Li and Liang (2021), we train our models on 10%, 20%, 30%, 50%, 70%, and 100% of the DailyDialog dataset to observe how the number of training samples affects the performance. We keep the validation and test sets full-sized for all experiments. For full experimental details, see App. B.

Metrics. We follow Li et al. (2017) and evaluate the models using BLEU4 score. Since we do not want the model to simply repeat the responses it has memorised from the training data, i.e. the dull response issue, we additionally introduce two new metrics: **novelty** and **diversity**. We define novelty as the proportion of model outputs on the test set that are not found in the training set. Given a test set, diversity is defined as the number of unique model outputs divided by the total number of outputs. A good dialog model should be able to achieve a high BLEU4 score, while maintaining a high level of novelty and diversity in its responses.

Models. We experiment with two models, DialoGPT (Zhang et al., 2020), a state-of-the-art dialog model, and GPT-2 (Radford et al., 2019) the model DialoGPT is fine-tuned from. We choose the latter model to gain insight into how useful in-domain pre-training of DialoGPT is for prompting.

5 Results

Our main results are contained in Fig. 3. First, we compare the performance of prompting vs fine-tuning on the DialoGPT model. We find that under the full data setting the dynamic prompt model outperforms the soft prompt model and even the fine-tuned model on all three metrics. With a BLEU4 of 0.12 dynamic prompt is 9% better than fine-tuning (0.11) and 15% better than a soft prompt (0.08). The difference is even more dramatic when we compare the corresponding diversity and novelty scores. Dynamic prompt achieves a novelty of 0.93 and diversity of 0.96, an improvement of 9% (0.85) and 10% (0.87) respectively over the soft prompt, and an even more pronounced improvement of 26% (0.74) and 22% (0.79) respectively over fine-tuning the model.

Next, we observe that soft-prompting is competitive in the low data setting and outperforms fine-tuning. However, with more than 30% of the training data available, soft-prompting stops improving altogether and begins to under-perform the other models. Dynamic prompt on the other hand maintains the best BLEU4 score no matter the amount of training data.

Now we turn to the question of novelty and diversity degradation. We observe that the dynamic prompt does not suffer from this issue nearly as much as the other models. In contrast, for the soft-prompted and fine-tuned models, the better the BLEU4 score gets the lower the novelty drops. While soft prompt already mitigates this drop-off, degrading slower than DialoGPT, dynamic prompt does not suffer from this effect and maintains above 90% novelty throughout. Similarly, for diversity, the dynamic prompt maintains around 0.95 score for any percentage of training data, while the soft prompt drops down over time and fine-tuning hovers around 0.80.

Finally, we can turn to the comparison of DialoGPT and GPT-2. Against our expectations, DialoGPT under-performs GPT-2 on BLEU4 despite the former having been pre-trained on dialog-specific data. The performance improvement is most notable in the case of the dynamic prompt, where GPT-2 (0.14) achieves 19% higher performance than DialoGPT (0.12). On the other hand, fine-tuning either model leads to nearly identical performance. You can find our discussion of this phenomenon in App. A, all our results in App. C and example outputs in App. D.

6 Related Work

Our work builds on two strains of thought. First, we deal with the problem of dull responses in dialog modelling. Related work includes the use of reinforcement learning (Li et al., 2016b), latent variables (Cao and Clark, 2017) and decoding techniques to mitigate this issue (Li et al., 2016a).

Second, we build on the idea of continuous prompting, which was developed concurrently by Lester et al. (2021) and Li and Liang (2021). There are many variations of the prompting paradigm. For instance, we fine-tune the embeddings along with the prompts, but Liu et al. (2021b) tune the prompt with the full model. Schick and Schütze (2021b) on the other hand tune only the model, while keeping the prompt fixed.

7 Conclusion

We find dynamic-prompting bests fine-tuning by generating more novel and diverse responses with a higher BLEU score while training only a small portion of the DialoGPT/GPT-2 parameters. Thus proving itself as a useful method for mitigating dialog modelling issue of *dull* responses. Prompting the general purpose GPT-2 achieves much higher performance than prompting the specialist DialoGPT model, suggesting that for pre-training data, diversity is more valuable for dialog modelling than dialog-specific information.

References

Tom Brown, Benjamin Mann, Nick Ryder, Melanie Subbiah, Jared D Kaplan, Prafulla Dhariwal, Arvind Neelakantan, Pranav Shyam, Girish Sastry, Amanda Askell, Sandhini Agarwal, Ariel Herbert-Voss, Gretchen Krueger, Tom Henighan, Rewon Child, Aditya Ramesh, Daniel Ziegler, Jeffrey Wu, Clemens Winter, Chris Hesse, Mark Chen, Eric Sigler, Mateusz Litwin, Scott Gray, Benjamin Chess, Jack Clark, Christopher Berner, Sam McCandlish, Alec Radford, Ilya Sutskever, and Dario Amodei. 2020. Language models are few-shot learners. In *Advances in Neural Information Processing Systems*, volume 33, pages 1877–1901. Curran Associates, Inc.

Kris Cao and Stephen Clark. 2017. Latent variable dialogue models and their diversity. In *Proceedings of the 15th Conference of the European Chapter of the Association for Computational Linguistics: Volume 2, Short Papers*, pages 182–187, Valencia, Spain. Association for Computational Linguistics.

Xiaodong Gu, Kang Min Yoo, and Sang-Woo Lee. 2021. Response generation with context-aware prompt learning. *arXiv preprint arXiv:2111.02643*.

Brian Lester, Rami Al-Rfou, and Noah Constant. 2021. The power of scale for parameter-efficient prompt tuning. In *Proceedings of the 2021 Conference on Empirical Methods in Natural Language Processing*, pages 3045–3059, Online and Punta Cana, Dominican Republic. Association for Computational Linguistics.

Jiwei Li, Will Monroe, and Dan Jurafsky. 2016a. A simple, fast diverse decoding algorithm for neural generation. *CoRR*, abs/1611.08562.

Jiwei Li, Will Monroe, Alan Ritter, Dan Jurafsky, Michel Galley, and Jianfeng Gao. 2016b. Deep reinforcement learning for dialogue generation. In *Proceedings of the 2016 Conference on Empirical Methods in Natural Language Processing*, pages 1192–1202, Austin, Texas. Association for Computational Linguistics.

Xiang Lisa Li and Percy Liang. 2021. Prefix-tuning: Optimizing continuous prompts for generation. In *Proceedings of the 59th Annual Meeting of the Association for Computational Linguistics and the 11th International Joint Conference on Natural Language Processing (Volume 1: Long Papers)*, pages 4582–4597, Online. Association for Computational Linguistics.

Yanran Li, Hui Su, Xiaoyu Shen, Wenjie Li, Ziqiang Cao, and Shuzi Niu. 2017. DailyDialog: A manually labelled multi-turn dialogue dataset. In *Proceedings of the Eighth International Joint Conference on Natural Language Processing (Volume 1: Long Papers)*, pages 986–995, Taipei, Taiwan. Asian Federation of Natural Language Processing.

Pengfei Liu, Weizhe Yuan, Jinlan Fu, Zhengbao Jiang, Hiroaki Hayashi, and Graham Neubig. 2021a. Pre-train, prompt, and predict: A systematic survey of prompting methods in natural language processing.

Xiao Liu, Yanan Zheng, Zhengxiao Du, Ming Ding, Yujie Qian, Zhilin Yang, and Jie Tang. 2021b. GPT understands, too. *arXiv preprint arXiv:2111.02643*.

Alec Radford, Jeffrey Wu, Rewon Child, David Luan, Dario Amodei, and Ilya Sutskever. 2019. Language models are unsupervised multitask learners.

Michael Rescorla. The language of thought hypothesis. In Edward N. Zalta, editor, *The Stanford Encyclopedia of Philosophy*.

Timo Schick and Hinrich Schütze. 2021a. Exploiting cloze-questions for few-shot text classification and natural language inference. In *Proceedings of the 16th Conference of the European Chapter of the Association for Computational Linguistics: Main Volume*, pages 255–269, Online. Association for Computational Linguistics.

Timo Schick and Hinrich Schütze. 2021b. It's not just size that matters: Small language models are also few-shot learners. In *Proceedings of the 2021 Conference of the North American Chapter of the Association for Computational Linguistics: Human Language Technologies*, pages 2339–2352, Online. Association for Computational Linguistics.

Iulian V. Serban, Alessandro Sordoni, Yoshua Bengio, Aaron Courville, and Joelle Pineau. 2016. Building end-to-end dialogue systems using generative hierarchical neural network models. In *Proceedings of the Thirtieth AAAI Conference on Artificial Intelligence*, AAAI'16, page 3776–3783. AAAI Press.

Alessandro Sordoni, Michel Galley, Michael Auli, Chris Brockett, Yangfeng Ji, Margaret Mitchell, Jian-Yun Nie, Jianfeng Gao, and Bill Dolan. 2015. A neural network approach to context-sensitive generation of conversational responses. In *Proceedings of the 2015 Conference of the North American Chapter of the Association for Computational Linguistics: Human Language Technologies*, pages 196–205, Denver, Colorado. Association for Computational Linguistics.

Yizhe Zhang, Siqi Sun, Michel Galley, Yen-Chun Chen, Chris Brockett, Xiang Gao, Jianfeng Gao, Jingjing Liu, and Bill Dolan. 2020. DIALOGPT : Large-scale generative pre-training for conversational response generation. In *Proceedings of the 58th Annual Meeting of the Association for Computational Linguistics: System Demonstrations*, pages 270–278, Online. Association for Computational Linguistics.

Tiancheng Zhao, Ran Zhao, and Maxine Eskenazi. 2017. Learning discourse-level diversity for neural dialog models using conditional variational autoencoders. In *Proceedings of the 55th Annual Meeting of the Association for Computational Linguistics*

(Volume 1: Long Papers), pages 654–664, Vancouver, Canada. Association for Computational Linguistics.

A Appendix A: Discussion

Liu et al. (2021a) designed their soft prompt based on the observation that context can control the LLM without the need to change its parameters. They demonstrate that the context might be hard to find among the existing word embeddings and instead learn it via back-propagation. We go a step further and demonstrate that when it comes to dialog generation it is harder to learn a single prompt than to learn a function that conditions the prompt on the query. We believe that this is because there is no single context, represented by words or embeddings, that can capture a complex task such as a conversation. This becomes intuitive if we separate the task of language generation from the task of making a conversation. The conversation is an interaction of the query with the state of the conversation agent. Without the ability to respond to the query the agent/language model is simply saying whatever is the most probable response. A prompt can induce some general modification over this response, but there is no process by which the agent can react to the query. In our dynamic prompt setting, the agent, represented by the controller module, is allowed to learn how to respond to each query.

The separation of thought from language production is of course not a new idea. Under the language of thought hypothesis, *mentalese* is the language of thought (Rescorla). While similar to natural language in its compositional structure, mentalese is separate from language itself. From this perspective, building models that separate the task of learning a language from that of learning how to use language makes perfect sense. Following this intuition, it also makes sense to pre-train the language model on general language, rather than a specific task. We believe that in our setting, the superior language ability of GPT-2 allows for a better Controller in the dynamic prompt setting.

B Appendix B: Experimental Details

We implement our models using the Pytorch and Huggingface libraries. We experiment with total of 36 configurations, testing three learning methods (Fine-tuning, Soft-prompting and Dynamic-prompting) on two LLMs (DialoGPT and GPT-2) and six data regimes (10%, 20%, 30%, 50%, 70%, and 100%). In each configuration, we run 12 trials of different learning rates $\in [3 \times 10^{-6}, 0.009]$, with a batch size of 8, for a maximum of 300 epochs (with early stopping after 100 epochs), and select the best model by validation BLEU. Each trial is done on a single GPU with 32GB memory, and the maximum training time is 14 days. To generate the model output, we always use only greedy decoding.

C Appendix C: Full Results

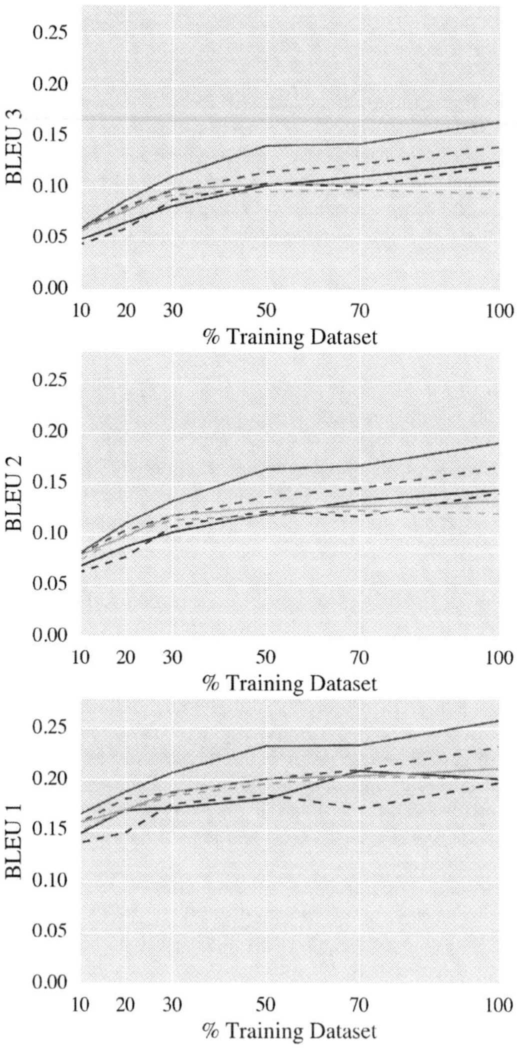

Figure 3: BLEU scores for **fine-tuning**, **soft-prompting** and **dynamic-prompting**. Full line is GPT-2, dashed line is DialoGPT.

Data	Model	BLEU1	BLEU2	BLEU3	BLEU4	Novelty	Diversity
10%	fine-tuning	0.138	0.063	0.044	0.034	0.850	0.732
	soft-prompting	0.149	0.075	0.057	0.046	0.908	0.895
	dynamic-prompting	0.158	0.081	0.060	0.048	0.902	0.889
20%	fine-tuning	0.148	0.078	0.060	0.050	0.827	0.764
	soft-prompting	0.170	0.100	0.080	0.067	0.921	0.926
	dynamic-prompting	0.181	0.104	0.082	0.068	0.942	0.941
30%	fine-tuning	0.176	0.108	0.088	0.075	0.810	0.809
	soft-prompting	0.184	0.114	0.093	0.078	0.921	0.928
	dynamic-prompting	0.187	0.118	0.097	0.082	0.940	0.944
50%	fine-tuning	0.185	0.123	0.104	0.090	0.791	0.813
	soft-prompting	0.196	0.119	0.096	0.080	0.884	0.903
	dynamic-prompting	0.201	0.137	0.115	0.098	0.939	0.952
70%	fine-tuning	0.172	0.118	0.101	0.089	0.714	0.756
	soft-prompting	0.204	0.124	0.098	0.080	0.869	0.889
	dynamic-prompting	0.210	0.146	0.123	0.104	0.930	0.958
100%	fine-tuning	0.197	0.141	0.122	0.109	0.737	0.787
	soft-prompting	0.201	0.121	0.094	0.076	0.847	0.874
	dynamic-prompting	0.232	0.166	0.140	0.119	0.933	0.961

Table 1: The full results of our experiments on DailyDialogue with DialoGPT.

Data	Model	BLEU1	BLEU2	BLEU3	BLEU4	Novelty	Diversity
10%	fine-tuning	0.147	0.069	0.049	0.039	0.910	0.852
	soft-prompting	0.158	0.080	0.060	0.048	0.910	0.903
	dynamic-prompting	0.166	0.082	0.060	0.047	0.939	0.917
20%	fine-tuning	0.170	0.088	0.066	0.054	0.903	0.856
	soft-prompting	0.170	0.098	0.077	0.065	0.881	0.878
	dynamic-prompting	0.188	0.111	0.088	0.074	0.930	0.932
30%	fine-tuning	0.172	0.102	0.082	0.070	0.855	0.837
	soft-prompting	0.188	0.119	0.099	0.084	0.906	0.916
	dynamic-prompting	0.207	0.133	0.111	0.095	0.923	0.934
50%	fine-tuning	0.181	0.120	0.102	0.089	0.806	0.799
	soft-prompting	0.201	0.127	0.103	0.087	0.873	0.902
	dynamic-prompting	0.233	0.164	0.141	0.124	0.924	0.947
70%	fine-tuning	0.209	0.134	0.111	0.095	0.883	0.900
	soft-prompting	0.204	0.128	0.103	0.086	0.897	0.917
	dynamic-prompting	0.234	0.168	0.143	0.124	0.912	0.946
100%	fine-tuning	0.201	0.144	0.125	0.111	0.742	0.801
	soft-prompting	0.211	0.133	0.106	0.087	0.845	0.874
	dynamic-prompting	0.258	0.190	0.164	0.142	0.913	0.944

Table 2: The full results of our experiments on DailyDialogue with GPT-2.

D Appendix D: Examples

Query	Dynamic-prompting	Fine-tuning	Soft-prompting
I think it unwise for either of us to be inflexible. How about meeting each other halfway?	Do I know how to meet these employees?	Then, what's your countr-offer?	That's verywise for either of us. How about meeting another person in person?
It's a success all right. The kids keep trying to catch me.	You better attach some good ones too.	I'm getting more and more special.	I'm glad you're here.
You can audition music on line, and you can audition it off line after downloading it, so you needn't pay for it.	But when I am getting done I will make a big fan list.	Is that a lot of people's music here?	Actually, I have been thinking about taking the notes from the book.
What date would you like to fly? Saturday, July 25. How many people will be traveling?	You'd better get a lot of tickets first.	A few people are coming to get me.	Two flight attendants will be coming with you.
It's more violent than TV news! What time is it anyway?	I don't know, but you are still beating around the bush. You aren't going to be able to stop anybody who looks like you.	Oh, man! I didn't notice it.	It's after ten o'clock, after the candles, so it's hard for me to make a decision.

Table 3: Example responses generated by the models under consideration. Red indicates reused training data response.

Most Language Models can be Poets too: An AI Writing Assistant and Constrained Text Generation Studio

Allen Roush Oracle Corporation
Sanjay Basu Oracle Corporation
Akshay Moorthy University of Oregon
Dmitry Dubovoy University of Oregon
allen.roush@oracle.com, sanjay.basu@oracle.com,
AkshayMoorthy123@gmail.com, ddubovoy@protonmail.com

Abstract

Despite rapid advancement in the field of Constrained Natural Language Generation, little time has been spent on exploring the potential of language models which have had their vocabularies lexically, semantically, and/or phonetically constrained. We find that most language models generate compelling text even under significant constraints. We present a simple and universally applicable technique for modifying the output of a language model by compositionally applying filter functions to the language models vocabulary before a unit of text is generated. This approach is plug-and-play and requires no modification to the model. To showcase the value of this technique, we present an easy to use AI writing assistant called "Constrained Text Generation Studio" (CTGS). CTGS allows users to generate or choose from text with any combination of a wide variety of constraints, such as banning a particular letter, forcing the generated words to have a certain number of syllables, and/or forcing the words to be partial anagrams of another word. We introduce a novel dataset of prose that omits the letter "e". We show that our method results in strictly superior performance compared to fine-tuning alone on this dataset. We also present a Huggingface "space" web-app presenting this technique called Gadsby. The code is available to the public here: https://github.com/Hellisotherpeople/Constrained-Text-Generation-Studio

1 Introduction

Constrained writing is a literary approach in which the writer decides to impose patterns, constraints, or conditions on their text. The most obvious example of this application is within poetry – but many other communities of writers also find imposing constraints on themselves to be enjoyable. We can divide constraints into two types, *soft-constraints* and *hard-constraints*.

Soft constraints are the kind that are fuzzy, e.g. deciding to write in a certain style. Soft constraints are almost exclusively applied at the sequence level, rather than being applied directly on each token. Hard constraints are concrete lexical, semantic, or phonetic requirements about the contents of a token or sequence. In this paper, we are presenting a system that applied token level hard-constraints to large-scale language models.

One notable group who create hard-constrained texts are the *Oulipo* (short for Ouvroir de littérature potentielle; roughly translated as the "workshop of potential literature") writing collective. Oulipo affiliated writers have produced a prolific amount of constrained literature since the 1960s. Oulipos founder has described the writers within the collective as "rats who construct the labyrinth from which they plan to escape".

One does not need to be a rodent to find "recreational linguistics" useful. Any suitor who has pledged their affection in print can attest to how difficult it can be to write good love poetry; and being able to generate rhyming text that also has the lengths of consecutive words matching the digits of pi is sure to swoon all but the most frigid of mathematicians.

Natural Language Generation has advanced at a breakneck pace. As models have scaled up, their

Proceedings of the 2nd Workshop on When Creative AI Meets Conversational AI (CAI2), COLING 2022, pages 9–15
October 12–17, 2022.

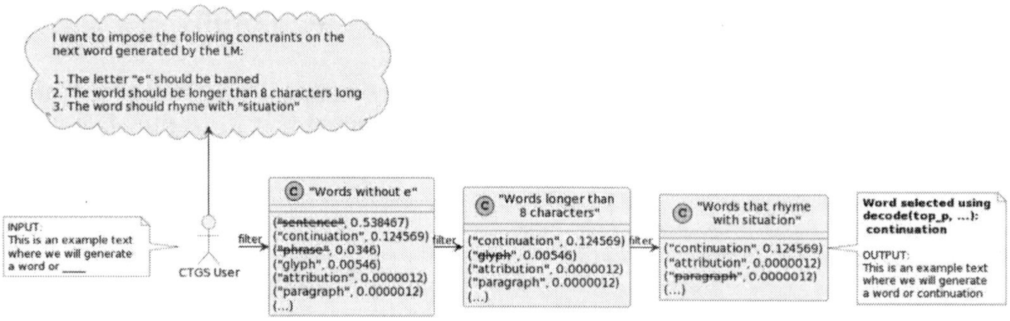

Figure 1: A use-case diagram of the algorithm

performance on a wide variety of tasks has improved. More recent work shows that sufficiently large models such as the "Pathways Language Model" (Chowdhery et al., 2022) unlock new capabilities for common sense reasoning. The probabilistic nature of language models makes their impressive performance particularly intriguing.

Ultimately, all language models involve some form of sampling from their vocabulary of all possible tokens that they could generate. In this paper, we explore the idea of adding arbitrarily compositional lexical, semantic, and/or phonetic filters to the crucial step of a language model sampling from its vocabulary during its decoding phase. Among other things, we observe that language models can remain coherent even with a remarkable amount of filters applied to their vocabulary. We thus find that it is perfectly appropriate to expect coherent output from a model like GPT-2 (Radford et al., 2019), when, for instance, its vocabulary is filtered to ban any word with the letter "e", the letter "a" is forced to appear, and the length of the token must be longer than 3.

In this paper, we introduce two systems which take advantage of this constrained vocabulary technique: An AI writing assistant called Constrained Text Generation Studio (CTGS) and a Huggingface "space" web-app called "Gadsby"[1].

Constrained Text Generation Studio is a GUI tool for recreational linguists, poets, creative writers, and/or researchers to use and study the ability of large-scale language models to recommend relevant text in nearly any situation. After specifying and downloading one of the thousands of language models made available on the Huggingface model hub, users can use CTGS to specify a list of constraints or "filters" that the vocabulary of the language model must pass through before it can be sampled from. After any combination of the filters are specified, users can either use traditional decoding methods to generate tokens from the constrained vocabulary automatically, or they can manually select their continuation from the list of valid tokens. CTGS was created with the idea of being "like Photoshop but for Constrained Text Generation".

Gadsby is a Huggingface hosted webapp which demonstrates the ability for language models to generate coherent text with several different pre-selected combinations of filters. Gadsby was named after one the most famous constrained works of fiction, which is a 270 page book written without the letter E. Gadsby is missing features that CTGS has, including composability of filters, optional human selection of continuations, and text transforms – but it includes filter pre-sets to showcase the robustness of language models to constraints. The most notable of these pre-sets is called "E-Prime"[2], which filters the specified language models vocabulary to avoid any form of the verb "to be".

2 Prior Work

We are not the first to explore Constrained Natural Language Generation with Language Models. Probably the closest prior work to our own comes

[1] Available here: https://huggingface.co/spaces/Hellisotherpeople/Gadsby

[2] The wikipedia article about this is fascinating: https://en.wikipedia.org/wiki/E-Prime

from Pascual et al. (2021). They propose a single plug-and-play semantic filter which shifts the sampling probabilities of a language models vocabulary towards a user defined keyword or set of keywords. CTGS instead offers a rich array of compositional lexical, phonetic, and semantic filters, and it preserves the original language models sampling probabilities with the exception of the filtered out tokens, which are banned.

Swanson et al. (2014) show that language models using Constrained Beam Search can effectively generate text with the constraint of either banning or requiring certain words to appear in a sequence. Notably, the transformers library from Huggingface recently integrated this functionality [3] . Constrained Beam Search is effective for translation and other sequence-to-sequence tasks, but it makes it impossible for the language model to assist humans on a per-token basis. CTGS adopts an optional human-in-the-loop approach where the user can decide which token to choose following the listed constraints at each step, rather than necessarily relying on sampling. Given the inherit creativity required for Constrained Writing, using language models for inspiration rather than blindly generating with them is uniquely helpful for recreational linguists.

Kumar et al. (2021) propose a method for Controlled Text Generation by formulating it as an optimization problem given a list of constraints and using gradient descent to maximize the log probability of the language model as well as the constraint objectives. The constraints that they provide are exclusively sequence level. By contrast, CTGS's filters are at the token level and are correspondingly much more appropriate for Oulipo or Poetry. Their method also requires a potentially lengthy optimization process.

Lu et al. (2021) propose a reinforcement learning based technique for generating sequences with conceptual constraints. This method requires training and is not applicable for hard lexical or phonetic constraints.

Zhang et al. (2020) developed a technique for solving the problem of hard-constraint generation. They propose to pre-train a model by progressively inserting tokens between existing tokens in a parallel manner. They introduce a large scale language model pre-trained this way and which is fine-tuned on hard-constrained tasks called POINTER. Their work only looks at the constraint of requiring certain words to appear in a sequence. Our work explores a wide variety of constraints and requires no training.

Other work related to constrained text generation which explores the potential of global constraint satisfaction at the sequence level comes from Mireshghallah et al. (2022). Surrogate models, such as BertScore, enforce these global constraints. Our writing assistant enforces constraints at the local level, and allows human intervention at any point.

Some intriguing work from the Task Oriented Dialogue community has parallels with our work. Balakrishnan et al. (2019) showcase how constrained decoding can be obtained by controlled modification of the model representation. They find that this technique improves semantic correctness as measured on the weather dataset.

3 Implementation Details

In this section, we explore the quirks, caveats, and details of the implementation of our technique within CTGS.

3.1 Filters

To enable a filter, a user checks the corresponding box, which will cause a larger group of settings to become visible. These settings are specific to each individual filter. After the relevant settings are specified, the button at the bottom of the settings enables the filter, and a list of filters which are enabled is shown at the top of the filters window.

CTGS at the time of writing includes 21 filters. Many of these filters are lexical, such as constraints which ban or force particular letters. Other filters are distance based, such as the semantic filter, which uses an auxiliary fasttext (Bojanowski, et al., 2016) model to remove language model vocabulary tokens which don't meet or exceed the specified semantic similarity threshold with a user supplied word.

Probably the most interesting of the included filters are phonetic in nature. CTGS includes filters for syllable count, meter, rhyme, and phonetic matching. CTGS achieves this feat by using the the

[3] An excellent blog post about this can be found here: https://huggingface.co/blog/constrained-beam-search

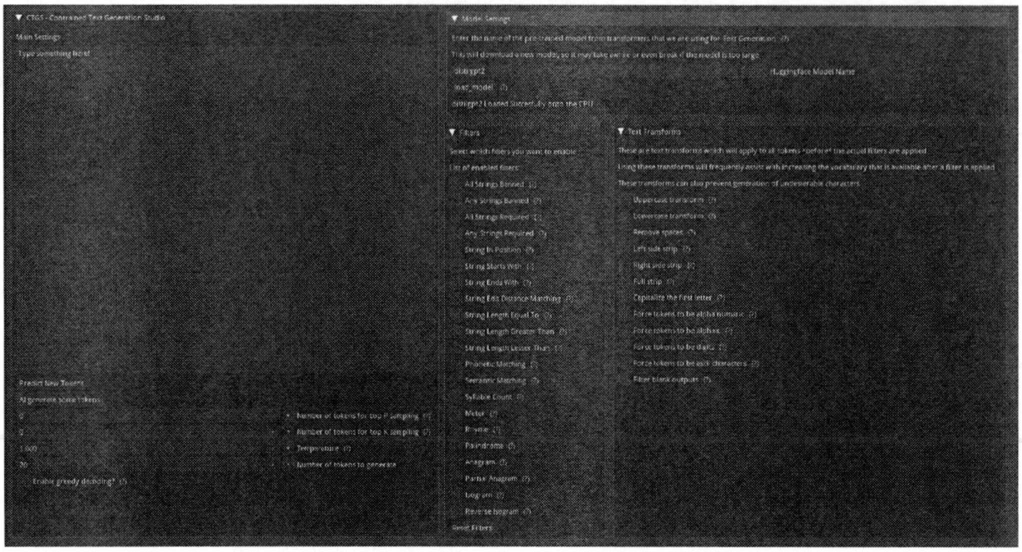

Figure 2: CTGS with the "Distilled-GPT2" (distilgpt2) model loaded. Users can right click within the textbox for a list of all possible continuations matching the currently selected filters

Carnegie Mellon Pronouncing Dictionary (CMUdict)[4]. The "double metaphone" phonetic algorithm is used for direct phonetic matching. These sorts of filters unlock the potential for poetry generation by large-scale language models since the rhyme, syllable, or meter constraints inherit to poetry are directly forced within the language models vocabulary.

3.2 Tokenization

Most of the constraints have the additional unpleasant side-effect of subverting the intention and value of subword tokenization schemes. This is because the filters assume that a language model generates its words all in one-step. Subword tokenization became the de facto default for large language models because increasing the vocabulary size of a language model dramatically increases the computational and memory footprint of the model. As the size and sophistication of language models has gone up, their vocabulary sizes have stayed constant[5]. This is frustrating for our technique, which naively assumes that a filter can be applied to a subword – an assumption which is often not true.

Unfortunately, most Language Models don't "signpost" as to whether they are generating a full word or a subword, requiring heuristic techniques to be used if one wanted to construct a "subword aware" filter. Even more startlingly, we observe that language models occasionally generate functionally *the same continuation* with subwords that they could have generated with direct words found within the vocabulary. Many of the filters in CTGS will absolutely cripple a language models ability to generate rare words which would be vectorized into subwords by the language models tokenizer. CTGS in its current form thrives when it is using a language model with a huge vocabulary.

Luckily, modern language models with huge vocabularies exists. One of these is "Transformer-XL", which showcased the value of using a word-tokenizer and an autoregressive architecture for generating coherent text (Dai et al., 2019). Its word-tokenizer doesn't leverage sub words, and thus these models do not succumb into the previously discussed issues. The default pre-trained models that Dai et al made available have a vocabulary size of 267735 tokens. That's a 5.32x increase in size over GPT-3! Unfortunately, one must also incur a significant penalty in memory and compute costs for this privilege.

4 Dataset without the "e"

One of the issues that large language models present for constrained writers is that even when heavily fine-tuned on a particular dataset, they

[4] Available here: https://github.com/cmusphinx/cmudict

[5] E.g. GPT, GPT-2, and GPT-3 all have a vocab size of 50257 words.

frequently *ignore their constraints*. For example, poetry models that were fine-tuned on the works of William Shakespeare frequently stumble and fail to maintain rhyme or meter.[6] We show that language models, which are fine-tuned even on the simple lexical constraint of omitting the letter "e", still occasionally ignore their constraints. In fact, even when these models are overtrained to an absurd degree, complete adherence to these constraints is unlikely.

Such behavior motivates the creation of datasets which include some forms of hard lexical, semantic, or phonetic constraints. By doing so, we can measure how often language models ignore them, and more importantly, we can show that this method of filtering out these tokens before the generation step leads to strictly better performance and eliminates these kinds of errors.

We present a dataset, called "Lipogram-e", which consists of all known complete book-length English works which do not use the letter "e". This dataset includes all of *Gadsby* by Ernest Vincent Wright, all of *A Void* by Georges Perec, and almost all of *Eunoia* by Christian Bok[7]. We name it "Lipogram-e" because a lipogram is a text where the author omits one or more letters from the alphabet.

While it may be possible to produce a dataset without the letter "e" by simply computationally looking through an existing large scale dataset for sentences which match that constraint, doing so would result in jumbled and incoherent training examples, with little relation to each other. By contrast, books and prose written with constraints have clear, coherent narratives. We chose the constraint of banning "e" because it is extremely easy to computationally verify and because there is no potential for error from the filter function.

5 Experiment

We design the experiment to measure how often a language model makes constraint-based mistakes on the Lipogram-e dataset. We look at the perplexity and the ignored constraint error rate of GPT-2-medium. We choose GPT-2-medium because of its relatively well-understood fine-tunability. We compare the untrained GPT-2 model to the regularly fine-tuned model, and the over-fine-tuned model. We show that in all instances, applying the constraint to ban the letter "e" from the vocabulary of these models results in both improved perplexity, as well as zero ignored constraint errors.

Model	Perplexity on test split	Ignored Constraint Error %
GPT-2	237.37	28.2
GPT-2 with constraint filter	**211.53**	**0**
GPT-2 fine-tuned for 5 epochs	78.24	0.5
GPT-2 fine-tuned for 5 epochs with constraint filter	**77.99**	**0**
GPT-2 fine-tuned for 20 epochs	75.58	0.3
GPT-2 fine-tuned for 20 epochs with constraint filter	**75.10**	**0**

Table 1: Results of the experiment on the Lipogram-e dataset

6 Discussion and Observations

Language models that have had their vocabularies filtered act significantly differently from unaltered models. Because the filters remove significant amounts of entries with high probability of being generated, models are more likely to behave undesirably. Some of the undesirable behavior observed included models generating total gibberish, generating repetitive text, generating potentially personally identifying information, generating profanity, and generating computer code. The more tokens which are filtered, and the higher their probability, the more likely it is that models will end up in these degenerate states. We hope that this paper motivates further and more exhaustive analysis of the vocabularies of language models and in particular, what properties they have when altered.

Filtering the vocabularies of language models opens up unique possibilities for adversarial machine learning. Any model which is exposing its full probability distribution before decoding could potentially be "attacked" by a sophisticated actor who has figured out what they "don't want" the

[6] An observation that has also been made by others: see here: https://www.gwern.net/GPT-2

[7] *Eunoia* is a work where each chapter only uses one vowel. We omit the chapter that uses the vowel "e"

model to generate. This could dramatically reduce the number of generations needed to leak specific information.

Similar techniques for filtering the output of all generative models could be explored in the future. Highly sophisticated text-to-image models like DALL-E from Ramesh et al. (2021) and Stable-Diffusion from Ho and Salimans (2021) might have interesting and unique behavior if pixel based filters that are analogous to our technique can be developed.

It would be extremely interesting to see how this technique will work with large scale language models such as OpenAIs GPT-3 or Huggingfaces BLOOM model. It is likely to make this technique extremely sophisticated, but large scale models frequently are not released to the public and their vocabularies probability distributions are not always exposed to the end user.

7 Final Thoughts and Conclusion

In this paper, we introduced the AI constrained writing assistant called CTGS, explained its features and rationale, and mused about its potential use cases. We also introduced a Huggingface hosted webapp which demonstrates the plug-and-play nature of constraining the vocabulary of a language model. We introduced a dataset of English books which do not contain the letter "e" called "Lipogram-e". We showed that our technique results in lower perplexity and zero ignored constraint errors in a variety of circumstances. Finally, we discussed the unique behaviors that models with constraints have.

We also hope to use this paper to serve as a call to action for the language modeling community to not abandon research into word level tokenizers and training models using them. If that's not possible, at least some form of "signposting" should be built into subsequently trained models using potentially a new subword tokenization scheme designed for this purpose. We hope this paper motivates future work on word-level tokenization, and on language models trained with extremely large vocabularies.

References

Balakrishnan, A., Rao, J., Upasani, K., White, M., and Subba, R. 2019. *Constrained Decoding for Neural NLG from Compositional Representations in Task-Oriented Dialogue.* ACL 2019 - 57th Annual Meeting of the Association for Computational Linguistics, Proceedings of the Conference, 831–844. Retrieved from http://arxiv.org/abs/1906.07220

Bojanowski, P., Grave, E., Joulin, A., and Mikolov, T. 2016. *Enriching Word Vectors with Subword Information.* Transactions of the Association for Computational Linguistics, *5*, 135–146. Retrieved from http://arxiv.org/abs/1607.04606

Chowdhery, A., Narang, S., Devlin, J., Bosma, M., Mishra, G., Roberts, A., … Fiedel, N. 2022. *PaLM: Scaling Language Modeling with Pathways.* Retrieved from http://arxiv.org/abs/2204.02311

Dai, Z., Yang, Z., Yang, Y., Carbonell, J., Le, Q. V., & Salakhutdinov, R. 2019. *Transformer-XL: Attentive Language Models Beyond a Fixed-Length Context*. ACL 2019 - 57th Annual Meeting of the Association for Computational Linguistics, Proceedings of the Conference, 2978–2988. Retrieved from http://arxiv.org/abs/1901.02860

Ho, Jonathan and Salimans, Tim, 2021, *Classifier-Free Diffusion Guidance*, NeurIPS 2021 Workshop on Deep Generative Models and Downstream Applications, Retrieved from https://arxiv.org/abs/2207.12598

Kumar, S., Malmi, E., Severyn, A., & Tsvetkov, Y. 2021. *Controlled Text Generation as Continuous Optimization with Multiple Constraints.* Retrieved from http://arxiv.org/abs/2108.01850

Lu, Y., Zhang, L., Han, W., Zhang, Y., & Tu, K. 2021. *Constrained Text Generation with Global Guidance-Case Study on CommonGen.*

Mireshghallah, F., Goyal, K., & Berg-Kirkpatrick, T. 2022. *Mix and Match: Learning-free Controllable Text Generation using Energy Language Models.* Retrieved from https://github.

Pascual, D., Egressy, B., Meister, C., Cotterell, R., and Wattenhofer, R. 2021. *A Plug-and-Play Method for Controlled Text Generation.* Retrieved from https://github.com/dapascual/K2T

Radford, A., Wu, J., Child, R., Luan, D., Amodei, D., and Sutskever, I. 2019. *Language Models are Unsupervised Multitask Learners.* Retrieved from https://github.com/codelucas/newspaper

Ramesh, Aditya and Pavlov, Mikhail and Goh, Gabriel and Gray, Scott and Voss, Chelsea and Radford, Alec and Chen, Mark and Sutskever, Ilya, 2021, *Zero-Shot Text-to-Image Generation.* Retrieved from https://arxiv.org/abs/2102.12092

Swanson, B., Yamangil, E., and Charniak, E. 2014. *Natural Language Generation with Vocabulary Constraints*.

Zhang, Y., Wang, G., Li, C., Gan, Z., Brockett, C., & Dolan, B. 2020. *POINTER: Constrained Progressive Text Generation via Insertion-based Generative Pre-training*. Retrieved from https://github.com/dreasysnail/POINTER

An Emotion-based Korean Multimodal Empathetic Dialogue System

Minyoung Jung*[1], Yeongbeom Lim*[1,2], San Kim[1], Jin Yea Jang[1], Saim Shin[1], and Ki-Hoon Lee[2]

[1]AIRC, Korea Electronics Technology Institute, South Korea
[2]School of Computer and Information Engineering, Kwangwoon University, South Korea
{minyoung.jung, warf34, kimsan0622, jinyea.jang, sishin}@keti.re.kr
kihoonlee@kw.ac.kr

Abstract

We propose a Korean multimodal dialogue system targeting emotion-based empathetic dialogues because most research in this field has been conducted in a few languages such as English and Japanese and in certain circumstances. Our dialogue system consists of an emotion detector, an empathetic response generator, a monitoring interface, a voice activity detector, a speech recognizer, a speech synthesizer, a gesture classification, and several controllers to provide both multimodality and empathy during a conversation between a human and a machine. For comparisons across visual influence on users, our dialogue system contains two versions of the user interface, a cat face-based user interface and an avatar-based user interface. We evaluated our dialogue system by investigating the dialogues in text and the average mean opinion scores under three different visual conditions, no visual, the cat face-based, and the avatar-based expressions. The experimental results stand for the importance of adequate visual expressions according to user utterances.

1 Introduction

As dialogue systems for human-machine conversations have attracted attention from the public, various multimodal dialogue systems with the purpose of healthcare (Wada and Shibata, 2007), empathetic conversation (Ishii et al., 2021) or multiparty attentive listening (Inoue et al., 2021b) have been recently introduced because multimodality makes conversations more entertaining (Pollmann et al., 2020). Most research in this field has been conducted by few research groups in industry or university because of the complicated architecture inherent in multimodal dialogue systems to control multimodal recognition or representation. Consequently, most multimodal dialogue systems are limited to a few languages such as English and Japanese.

Empathy is also the main factor for more humanized conversation (Zech and Rimé, 2005) along with multimodality. Researches on empathetic dialogues (Lin et al., 2020; Zheng et al., 2021; Zhong et al., 2020; Li et al., 2021; Kim et al., 2021a; Sabour et al., 2022) are also focused on a few languages from a lack of empathetic dialogue datasets. Although a Korean empathetic dataset (Yang et al., 2020) and a Korean empathetic dialogue generation model (Jang et al., 2022) have been recently published, a Korean empathetic dialogue system supporting multimodality has not been studied.

This paper makes the following contributions:

1. We propose an emotion-based Korean multimodal empathetic dialogue system composed of an emotion detector, an empathetic response generator, a monitoring interface, a voice activity detector, a speech recognizer, a speech synthesizer, a gesture classification, and several controllers.

2. We provide three different visual-representing conditions to compare the user's behaviors and opinion scores. The three conditions include no visualization (a black screen), a cat face-based emotion expression, and an avatar-based gesture expression.

3. We evaluate our dialogue system with six participants collected for our experiments. The experiments are performed under three different visual-expressing conditions. We analyze the experimental results which are dialogues in text form and average mean opinion scores.

The remainder of this paper is formed as follows. We explain our emotion-based Korean multimodal empathetic dialogue system in Section 2. In Section 3, the experimental results of our dialogue system are discussed. Section 4 contains the related

*Equal contribution

Proceedings of the 2nd Workshop on When Creative AI Meets Conversational AI (CAI2), COLING 2022, pages 16–22
October 12–17, 2022.

work in multimodal dialogue systems and empathetic dialogues. Finally, we draw our conclusion in Section 5.

2 Empathetic Dialogue System

We illustrate the emotion-based Korean multimodal empathetic dialogue system. As shown in Fig. 1, the overall architecture of the dialogue system is composed of modules on a device and server(s). The device must be equipped with at least a microphone, a speaker, a display, and a computer for voice activity detection, speech recognition, speech synthesis, and visual expression. The visual expression is derived from either a cat face-based emotion expression (V1) or an avatar-based gesture expression (V2). The modules on server(s) are an emotion detector, an empathetic response generator, a monitoring service, and the main controller to receive inputs (user information and a user speech in text) from the device and to send outputs (a system response in text, a detected emotion class, and estimated probabilities of a user emotion and a system dialogue strategy) to the device. Those modules can operate on the device instead of server(s) if the computing and memory resources on the device afford them. Otherwise, they can be executed on a single server or several servers in consideration of the resources on the server(s).

2.1 Emotion Classification Model

For generating more empathetic responses, utilization of user emotions is essential. Therefore we need an emotion classification model recognizing the user's emotion from the current user utterance among happy, sad, fear/anxiety, angry, surprise, disgust, and neutral in accordance with Ekman's six basic emotions (Ekman, 1992). The text emotion classification model (Lim et al., 2021) on the basis of Korean-English T5 (KE-T5) (Kim et al., 2021b), a T5 (Raffel et al., 2020)-based pre-trained model for both English and Korean, is adopted as the emotion detection model in our architecture. And the emotion detection model is re-trained on the extended version of the Korean empathetic conversation corpus (Yang et al., 2020) because the dataset used in (Lim et al., 2021) is on the basis of eight emotions.

2.2 Dialogue Generation Model

The dialogue generation model aims to automatically generate system responses in an empathetic manner, based on the latest three user utterances by utilizing the user emotion and the system's dialogue strategy. The user emotion is decided among the seven emotions as defined in Section 2.1, and the system dialogue strategy is determined among clarification, back-channel, facilitation, approval, disapproval, surprise, encouragement, evaluation, echoic, greeting, opinion, suggestion, and persona according to the extended version of the Korean empathetic conversation corpus (Yang et al., 2020). The KE-T5-based empathetic dialogue model (Jang et al., 2022) is employed as the empathetic response generation model in our architecture after the model is re-trained on the extended version of the Korean empathetic conversation corpus (Yang et al., 2020) because the persona class is added to the strategy classes.

2.3 User Interface

For human-machine multimodal interaction, we provide two versions of a user interface which are a cat face-based and an avatar-based user interface. Whenever our empathetic dialogue system starts, either of them can be chosen to deliver adequate visual-representation to the system responses. Both versions receive user information such as a user ID and user voice in speech. Once the user voice is detected, the speech recognition (speech to text) of the Web Speech API transforms the voice into the text so that emotion detection and empathetic response generation modules can obtain and process the text through the main controller on a server. After the emotion detection and empathetic response generation modules produce the recognized user emotion and the system response in the form of text, their outputs are sent to the chosen version of the user interface for the motion expression and the speech synthesis (text to speech).

2.3.1 Cat Face-Based User Interface

The first version (V1) of the user interface, a cat face-based Web user interface, receives the generated system response in text form and the detected user emotion for the speech synthesis and the emotion expression respectively. According to the emotion types in Section 2.1, seven different cat face-based motions are designed to express the user's emotion as shown in Fig. 2. The device can therefore provide the audio and visual interaction simultaneously to the user, through the audio controller and the emotion expression controller.

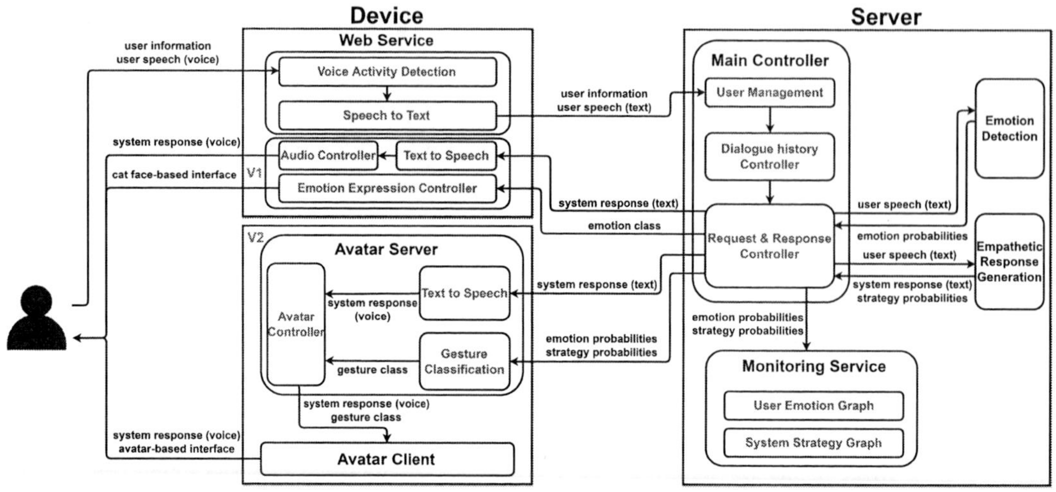

Figure 1: Overall architecture of our emotion-based Korean multimodal empathetic dialogue system

(a) Happy (b) Sad (c) Fear/Anxiety (d) Angry (e) Surprise (f) Disgust (g) Neutral

Figure 2: Seven different cat face-based motions

2.3.2 Avatar-Based User Interface

The second version (V2) of the user interface, an avatar-based Unity user interface, receives the generated system response in the form of text, the detected user emotion, and the suggested system dialogue strategy for speech synthesis and gesture expression. The current gesture classification module randomly selects a gesture from the seven different general-purpose avatar gestures as depicted in Fig. 3. The gestures include holding out one hand (A) or both hands (D), tilting (B) or nodding (E) the head, crossing the arms (C), and putting one hand (F) or both hands (G) on the chest. If some specific-purpose gestures are added afterward, the gesture classification module can utilize the given user emotion and system strategy to choose a more appropriate gesture for future work. The synthesized system voice in speech and the chosen gesture class are transmitted to the avatar controller so that the avatar server can send both information to the avatar client. Then the avatar client on the device can play the voice and gesture motion concurrently.

2.3.3 Monitoring Interface

The monitoring web interface is provided for participants so that they can check their current and some recent past emotions, and the current system dialogue strategy, as illustrated in Fig. 4. The x-axis and y-axis of the user emotion graph represent the time when the emotion is detected and the estimated emotion probabilities. And the system dialogue strategy probabilities are presented in the radial graph.

3 Experiments

For evaluating our emotion-based Korean multimodal empathetic dialogue system, we analyze the dialogue logs and the averaged mean opinion scores (MOS) achieved by six participants. MOS is commonly used to assess the dialogue system since no existing automatic evaluation metrics correctly measure the performance of the dialogue generation task. Our dialogue system was also evaluated in three different visual-representing conditions which are no visual (a black screen), the cat face-based, and the avatar-based expression methods.

3.1 Experimental Settings

A 160 cm kiosk built in a microphone, a speaker, a display, and a computer is employed for all our experiments conducted with six participants and

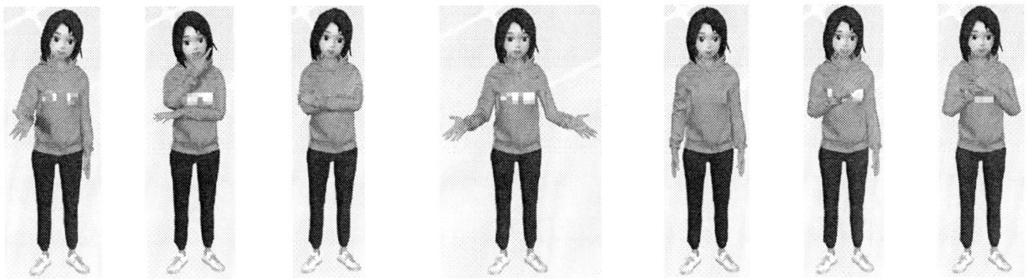

(a) Gesture A (b) Gesture B (c) Gesture C (d) Gesture D (e) Gesture E (f) Gesture F (g) Gesture G

Figure 3: Seven different general-purpose avatar gestures

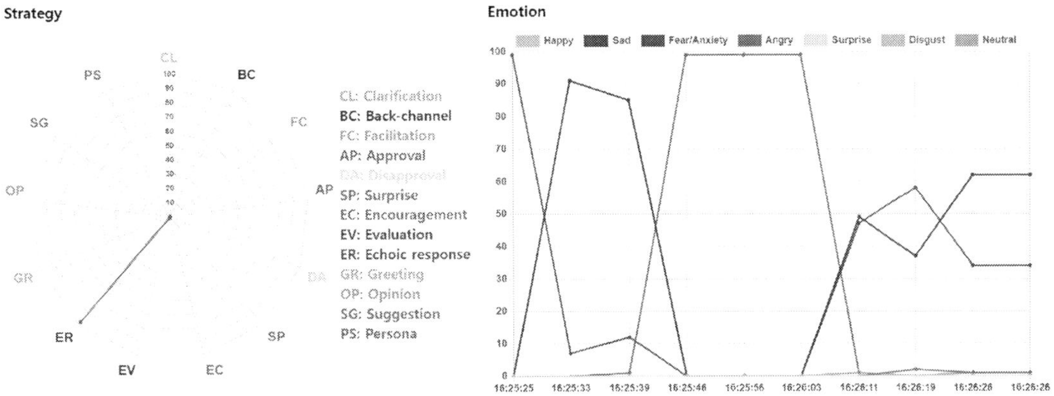

Figure 4: Monitoring interface drawing estimated probabilities of a current system strategy and latest user emotions

three visual expressing conditions. A participant starts a conversation with the kiosk given the condition, finishes the conversation when the participant wants, has a pause while other participants have a conversation with the kiosk, starts another conversation with the kiosk under another condition different from the first condition, and iterates the same steps until the participant tests all three visual conditions. The order of conditions given to each participant is randomly shuffled so that the evaluation results are not affected by the order.

For the speech synthesis, the Kakao text-to-speech API is selected because it provides a calm female voice in Korean, which sounds proper for most empathetic dialogues.

3.2 Experimental Results

For observing the changes in terms of participants' behavior, the dialogue logs were recorded individually depending on the participant and the visual condition. The numbers of user utterances per dialogue and words per user utterance are calculated on average, as shown in Table 1. The average number of words per user utterance for all three conditions is almost the same, whereas the users tend to talk less with the cat face and more with the avatar.

The participants graded each evaluation item on a 5-point scale from 1 to 5. A participant considers an evaluation item very bad if the participant scores 1 for the item, whereas scoring 5 means very good. The questionnaire was given to the participants before the experiment and contained the questions as described in Table 2. Except for Q4, all participants gave a mark for each conversation under a given visual condition. Question Q4 was only rated when no black screen was provided. We observed that the participants gave higher MOS with the cat face although we utilize the same emotion detector and the empathetic dialogue generator for all conditions. In case of question Q4, the participants considered that the emotion-based cat face expression was more proper than the random general purpose gesture-based avatar expression. The overall satisfaction scores (Q5) showed that the participants were the most satisfied with the cat face and the least satisfied with the avatar. The result that the avatar-based representation achieved lower MOS than the black screen implies the importance

Evaluation item	None	Cat face	Avatar
The average number of user utterances per dialogue	17.0	16.3	**18.3**
The average number of words per user utterance	3.8	4.0	4.0

Table 1: Average numbers of user utterances per dialogue and words per user utterance under three visual conditions

	Evaluation item	None	Cat face	Avatar
Q1	The recognized emotion was correct	**4.2**	**4.2**	**4.2**
Q2	The system strategy was appropriate	3.8	**4.0**	3.7
Q3	The system response was appropriate	**4.0**	**4.0**	3.3
Q4	The cat face or avatar gesture matched with the system response	n/a	**3.8**	2.8
Q5	The overall dialogue satisfied me	4.0	**4.2**	3.3

Table 2: Average mean opinion scores under three visual conditions

of providing appropriate visual-representation by understanding given user utterances.

4 Related Work

Several social robots providing multimodal interaction have been introduced for different purposes. The baby seal-shaped robot PARO was developed by the National Institute of Advanced Industrial Science and Technology in Japan for robot therapy (Wada and Shibata, 2007). And the PARO robot was utilized for examining whether the robot can support family caregivers caring for older persons with dementia (Inoue et al., 2021a). The Pepper robot, a wheeled humanoid robot produced by SoftBank Robotics, was initially designed for business-to-business in SoftBank stores and has been utilized for a variety of applications for business-to-consumer, business-to-academics, and business-to-developers (Pandey and Gelin, 2018). (Glas et al., 2016) created the ERICA robot, one of the most humanlike android robots, whose functionalities include conversation, advanced sensing, and speech synthesis. And the abilities of the ERICA robot extended into one-on-one attentive listening (Inoue et al., 2020) and multi-party attentive listening (Inoue et al., 2021b). The ERICA robot was also utilized for empathetic conversation during the Covid-19 quarantine (Ishii et al., 2021).

As empathy plays a crucial role in communication, there have been several attempts to generate more empathetic system responses in text-based conversations. An end-to-end empathetic chatbot CAiRE (Lin et al., 2020) recognizes user emotions and generates responses in an empathetic manner, based on the Generative Pre-trained Transformer (Radford et al., 2018). (Zheng et al., 2021) proposed a multi-factor hierarchical framework for empathetic response generation, which consists of communication mechanism, dialog act, and emotion. (Zhong et al., 2020) suggested a novel large-scale dataset (PEC) and a BERT (Devlin et al., 2019)-based response selection model for persona-based empathetic conversations. (Li et al., 2021) and (Kim et al., 2021a) focused on emotion causes for generating empathetic responses. (Sabour et al., 2022) leveraged commonsense to achieve additional information such as user's situations and feelings. And the information was utilized for the enhancement of empathetic response generation.

5 Conclusion

This paper proposes an emotion-based Korean multimodal empathetic dialogue system whose submodules include an emotion detector, an empathetic response generator, a monitoring interface, a web interface, and a unity interface. We evaluated our dialogue system by analyzing the dialogues in text and the average mean opinion scores under the three different visual-representing conditions and observed the significance of proper visual expressions. For future research, gesture classification with more specific-purpose gestures and system emotion expression corresponding to the system response will be considered.

Acknowledgements

This work was supported by Institute of Information & communications Technology Planning & Evaluation (IITP) grant funded by the Korea government(MSIT) (No. 2022-0-00320, Artificial intelligence research about cross-modal dialogue modeling for one-on-one multi-modal interactions)

References

Jacob Devlin, Ming-Wei Chang, Kenton Lee, and Kristina Toutanova. 2019. BERT: Pre-training of deep bidirectional transformers for language understanding. In *Proceedings of the 2019 Conference of the North American Chapter of the Association for Computational Linguistics: Human Language Technologies, Volume 1 (Long and Short Papers)*, pages 4171–4186, Minneapolis, Minnesota. Association for Computational Linguistics.

Paul Ekman. 1992. An argument for basic emotions. *Cognition and Emotion*, 6(3-4):169–200.

Dylan F. Glas, Takashi Minato, Carlos T. Ishi, Tatsuya Kawahara, and Hiroshi Ishiguro. 2016. Erica: The erato intelligent conversational android. In *2016 25th IEEE International Symposium on Robot and Human Interactive Communication (RO-MAN)*, pages 22–29.

Kaoru Inoue, Kazuyoshi Wada, and Takanori Shibata. 2021a. Exploring the applicability of the robotic seal paro to support caring for older persons with dementia within the home context. *Palliative Care and Social Practice*, 15:26323524211030285. PMID: 34350398.

Koji Inoue, Divesh Lala, Kenta Yamamoto, Shizuka Nakamura, Katsuya Takanashi, and Tatsuya Kawahara. 2020. An attentive listening system with android ERICA: Comparison of autonomous and WOZ interactions. In *Proceedings of the 21th Annual Meeting of the Special Interest Group on Discourse and Dialogue*, pages 118–127, 1st virtual meeting. Association for Computational Linguistics.

Koji Inoue, Hiromi Sakamoto, Kenta Yamamoto, Divesh Lala, and Tatsuya Kawahara. 2021b. A multi-party attentive listening robot which stimulates involvement from side participants. In *Proceedings of the 22nd Annual Meeting of the Special Interest Group on Discourse and Dialogue*, pages 261–264, Singapore and Online. Association for Computational Linguistics.

Etsuko Ishii, Genta Indra Winata, Samuel Cahyawijaya, Divesh Lala, Tatsuya Kawahara, and Pascale Fung. 2021. ERICA: An empathetic android companion for covid-19 quarantine. In *Proceedings of the 22nd Annual Meeting of the Special Interest Group on Discourse and Dialogue*, pages 257–260, Singapore and Online. Association for Computational Linguistics.

Jin Yea Jang, San Kim, Minyoung Jung, and Saim Shin. 2022. Utilization of emotions and strategies in generating system response of the empathetic dialogue models. In *ICEIC*.

Hyunwoo Kim, Byeongchang Kim, and Gunhee Kim. 2021a. Perspective-taking and pragmatics for generating empathetic responses focused on emotion causes. In *Proceedings of the 2021 Conference on Empirical Methods in Natural Language Processing*, pages 2227–2240, Online and Punta Cana, Dominican Republic. Association for Computational Linguistics.

San Kim, Jin Yea Jang, Minyoung Jung, and Saim Shin. 2021b. A model of cross-lingual knowledge-grounded response generation for open-domain dialogue systems. In *Findings of the Association for Computational Linguistics: EMNLP 2021*, pages 352–365, Punta Cana, Dominican Republic. Association for Computational Linguistics.

Yanran Li, Ke Li, Hongke Ning, Xiaoqiang Xia, Yalong Guo, Chen Wei, Jianwei Cui, and Bin Wang. 2021. Towards an online empathetic chatbot with emotion causes. In *Proceedings of the 44th International ACM SIGIR Conference on Research and Development in Information Retrieval*, SIGIR '21, pages 2041–2045, New York, NY, USA. Association for Computing Machinery.

Yeongbeom Lim, San Kim, Jin Yea Jang, Saim Shin, and Minyoung Jung. 2021. Ke-t5-based text emotion classification in korean conversations. In *HCLT*, pages 496–497.

Zhaojiang Lin, Peng Xu, Genta Indra Winata, Farhad Bin Siddique, Zihan Liu, Jamin Shin, and Pascale Fung. 2020. Caire: An end-to-end empathetic chatbot. *Proceedings of the AAAI Conference on Artificial Intelligence*, 34(09):13622–13623.

Amit Kumar Pandey and Rodolphe Gelin. 2018. A mass-produced sociable humanoid robot: Pepper: The first machine of its kind. *IEEE Robotics & Automation Magazine*, 25(3):40–48.

Kathrin Pollmann, Christopher Ruff, Kevin Vetter, and Gottfried Zimmermann. 2020. Robot vs. voice assistant: Is playing with pepper more fun than playing with alexa? In *Companion of the 2020 ACM/IEEE International Conference on Human-Robot Interaction*, HRI '20, pages 395–397, New York, NY, USA. Association for Computing Machinery.

Alec Radford, Karthik Narasimhan, Tim Salimans, Ilya Sutskever, et al. 2018. Improving language understanding by generative pre-training.

Colin Raffel, Noam Shazeer, Adam Roberts, Katherine Lee, Sharan Narang, Michael Matena, Yanqi Zhou, Wei Li, and Peter J. Liu. 2020. Exploring the limits of transfer learning with a unified text-to-text transformer. *Journal of Machine Learning Research*, 21(140):1–67.

Sahand Sabour, Chujie Zheng, and Minlie Huang. 2022. Cem: Commonsense-aware empathetic response generation. *Proceedings of the AAAI Conference on Artificial Intelligence*, 36(10):11229–11237.

Kazuyoshi Wada and Takanori Shibata. 2007. Living with seal robots—its sociopsychological and physiological influences on the elderly at a care house. *IEEE Transactions on Robotics*, 23(5):972–980.

Jae Hee Yang, Jin Yea Jang, Minyoung Jung, and Saim Shin. 2020. Establishing a corpus for an ai-based empathic response system. In *ICONI*.

Emmanuelle Zech and Bernard Rimé. 2005. Is talking about an emotional experience helpful? effects on emotional recovery and perceived benefits. *Clinical Psychology & Psychotherapy*, 12(4):270–287.

Chujie Zheng, Yong Liu, Wei Chen, Yongcai Leng, and Minlie Huang. 2021. CoMAE: A multi-factor hierarchical framework for empathetic response generation. In *Findings of the Association for Computational Linguistics: ACL-IJCNLP 2021*, pages 813–824, Online. Association for Computational Linguistics.

Peixiang Zhong, Chen Zhang, Hao Wang, Yong Liu, and Chunyan Miao. 2020. Towards persona-based empathetic conversational models. In *Proceedings of the 2020 Conference on Empirical Methods in Natural Language Processing (EMNLP)*, pages 6556–6566, Online. Association for Computational Linguistics.

BETOLD: A Task-Oriented Dialog Dataset for Breakdown Detection

Silvia Terragni, Bruna Guedes, Andre Manso,
Modestas Filipavicius, Nghia Khau and **Roland Mathis**
Telepathy Labs GmbH
Zürich, Switzerland
{firstname.lastname}@telepathy.ai

Abstract

Task-Oriented Dialog (TOD) systems often suffer from dialog breakdowns - situations in which users cannot or do not want to proceed with the conversation. Ideally TOD systems should be able to detect dialog breakdowns to prevent users from quitting a conversation and to encourage them to interact with the system again. In this paper, we present BETOLD, a privacy-preserving dataset for breakdown detection. The dataset consists of user and system turns represented by intents and entity annotations, derived from NLU and NLG dialog manager components. We also propose an attention-based model that detects potential breakdowns using these annotations, instead of the utterances' text. This approach achieves a comparable performance to the corresponding utterance-only model, while ensuring data privacy.

1 Introduction

Task-Oriented Dialog (TOD) systems (Zhang et al., 2020) enable users to complete specific tasks, such as booking a reservation at a restaurant. Unlike open-domain dialog systems (Huang et al., 2020), where the aim is to maximize user engagement, in TOD systems it is crucial to optimally assist a user to fulfill the task at hand. Detecting dialog breakdowns due to miscommunications potentially paves the way to intervene and rescue the dialog, improve customer satisfaction and motivate the user to continue interacting with the system (Brandtzæg and Følstad, 2018).

A dialog breakdown is often defined as a point in the dialog where the user gives up the conversation without completing the task, often due to not understanding the intended meaning of user's utterance (Martinovski and Traum, 2003; Higashinaka et al., 2015). If conversational system engineers can understand when and why a conversation is likely to break down, they can build systems that prevent broken dialogs, or design conversational breakdown recovery strategies (Benner et al., 2021).

The Dialog Breakdown Detection Challenge (DBDC) has motivated the academic community's interest in the breakdown detection problem, which is the goal of predicting the occurrence of a breakdown at some point in the conversation (Higashinaka et al., 2016). This challenge also came with the release of English and Japanese datasets for addressing this task. Despite the great value of these proposed datasets, they only provide the sequence of user and system utterances. Utterances are indeed useful to detect a breakdown, however, in certain contexts, especially in industry, a stakeholder may decide not to share and release the texts for privacy preserving purposes (Xu et al., 2021).

The utterances produced by a user during a task-oriented conversation often contain privacy-sensitive information. Let us consider a dialog system in a company that handles issues relating to human resources as an example. The system may receive data regarding an employee's health status or compensation, i.e., data that a company is unwilling to share. In this paper, we demonstrate that even without access to the text of the conversation, it is still possible to identify a breakdown. In fact, traditional dialog systems often provide synthetic annotation of the user and system utterances as the intents and entities, originating from the Natural Language Understanding (NLU) and Natural Language Generation (NLG) components (Wahde and Virgolin, 2022). In particular, the NLU component classifies the user utterances into intents (`book_appointment`) and extracts entities (`user_name="John Smith"`). The NLG component consists of a closed set of possible system utterances (each defined by a unique intent), often parameterized by or supplemented with entities (e.g. "`restaurant_name` is open on `day_of_the_week`", where `restaurant_name` and `day_of_the_week`

Proceedings of the 2nd Workshop on When Creative AI Meets Conversational AI (CAI2), COLING 2022, pages 23–34
October 12–17, 2022.

		BETOLD	DBDC	DSTC2
Annotation Features	Task-oriented dialogs	Yes	partially	Yes
	Task domain	phone repair	mixed	restaurant, tourist info
	Annotation by	automatic	human	human
	Has intents	Yes	Yes	Yes
	Has entities	Yes	No	Yes
Breakdown Features	BD* annotated by	system	human	human
	BD label	Yes	Yes	NO**
	BD defined as	caller hangup & transfer request	nonsensical system reply	inferred from intent
	Number of classes	2	3	2
	Partial BD label	No	Yes	No
	BD initiated by caller	Yes	No	Yes
System Abilities	ASR and TTS	Yes	No	No
Statistics	# Dialogs	13,524	615	2,115
	# utterances per dialog (median)	10	20	12

Table 1: Comparison of our BETOLD and other two publicly available datasets used for breakdown detection. *BD stands for "breakdown". **User's intent "restart" could be used as a substitute for breakdown.

are two entities).

In our study, we propose a simple yet effective way to *automatically* create a new breakdown detection dataset, given an existing TOD system. In particular, we consider a phone-call scenario, in which a customer talks to a digital assistant to schedule a service appointment for their mobile phone. In our experience, two central events indicating caller's frustration with the current dialog state and projected outcomes are: a) hang-ups, b) requests to talk to a human agent. Therefore, we consider caller hang-ups and transfer to human requests as dialog breakdowns.

We also release a novel task-oriented dialog dataset BETOLD (Breakdown Expectation for Task-Oriented Long Dialogues) with the proposed annotation schema. The dataset contains real human-agent conversations, between customers and our modular dialog system. The system automatically annotates the user utterances with NLU intents and entities, and generates appropriate NLG responses which contain NLG intents and accompanying entities.

Finally, we propose an attention-based model, capable of taking these features into account. Our results show that, instead of relying only on the word tokens of the utterances, the use of NLU and NLG intents is sufficient to confidently predict a breakdown in a task-oriented conversation, therefore reaching satisfactory results while guaranteeing the privacy of the data.

2 Related Work

2.1 Datasets for Breakdown Detection

Only few task-oriented dialog breakdown datasets are openly available. We report the most relevant ones in Table 1. Overall, they are small and human-annotated, and with varying definitions of dialog breakdown.

The Dialogue Breakdown Detection Challenge (DBDC) offers a small dataset with 615 English conversations, annotated with system utterances that cause dialog breakdown (Higashinaka et al., 2016). It contains three classes: breakdown, possible breakdown, and no breakdown. However, no intents and entities annotations are available. Additionally, opposite to BETOLD, most of conversations in DBDC are open-domain. Another open-source alternative is the Dialog State Tracking Challenge (DSTC2) dataset, which unfortunately lacks breakdown annotations (Williams et al., 2014). However, 7 out of 2,115 conversations have an intent "Restart" which. If more prevalent, this could be used as a substitute for breakdown.

Similar to our work, Gorin et al. (1997) annotated 10,000 TODs between customers and agents. Subsequent experiments with the same dataset identified user hangup and requests to transfer to human agent as a specific learning problem, as proposed in our work (Walker et al., 2000). However, the dataset is not publicly available. Further examples of closed-source studies feature predicting interaction quality from automatically extracted features (Schmitt et al., 2011) or manually-annotated features by AMT workers (Meena et al., 2015). These studies used publicly available un-annotated datasets, however the authors did not release their annotations.

2.2 Models for Breakdown Detection

The initial approaches to the breakdown identification problem focused on extracting features that can characterize a breakdown (Schmitt et al., 2011; Meena et al., 2015; Walker et al., 2000). Textual features can be used to compute similarity between the system utterance and user utterance (Meena et al., 2015), or detecting emotions from utterances and using them as indicators of a dialog breakdown (Schmitt et al., 2011; Matsumoto et al., 2022). Alternatively, dialog manager-generated tabular features such as repetitions, negations, or utterance counts can be considered as well (Walker et al., 2000; Schmitt et al., 2011).

With advent of the DBDC challenge, novel approaches have been proposed, yet limited by the available dataset features. These approaches rely solely on the textual utterances and the number of turns. They explore both traditional (Kato and Sakai, 2017; Sugiyama, 2021) and deep learning-based models (Hendriksen et al., 2021; Wang et al., 2021; Park et al., 2017). Given the sequential nature of dialogs, many models exploit sequential architectures, such as RNN or LSTM (Hendriksen et al., 2021; Wang et al., 2021; Shin et al., 2019; Lee et al., 2020), or they use an attention mechanism to determine the utterance embeddings on which to focus the attention (Park et al., 2017). Considering the encoding of the text, different approaches have been investigated: from the use of static word embeddings such as Glove and Word2Vec (Hendriksen et al., 2021) to contextualized embeddings, e.g., BERT (Sugiyama, 2021; Shin et al., 2019).

3 A Privacy-Preserving Dataset for Breakdown Detection

3.1 Dataset Creation

The considered conversations are based on real conversations between a human and a task-oriented dialog system, with the goal of scheduling or canceling an appointment. The user interacts with the system over the phone. We considered four scenarios in which a phone call could end:

- **successful calls**: the caller hangs up after the caller's goal has been satisfied (e.g. the agent has successfully scheduled a booking);
- **agent-initiated forwarded calls**: the agent takes the decision to forward the call (e.g. technical problems with the system);
- **user-initiated forwarded calls**: the user explicitly requests to talk to an operator, identified by the *transfer_to_human* intent. (This may include NLU misclassifications);
- **user-initiated caller hangup**: all the remaining calls.

A conversational engineer strives to avoid both user-initiated forward calls and user-initiated hangups. However, observing the data, we can see that the caller's behavior changes depending on the number of turns. There is no way to prevent the caller from hanging up in the initial turns: This is the case when a user does not want to speak to a digital assistant at all. We report in Figure 1 the distribution of the different types of phone calls over the number of turns.

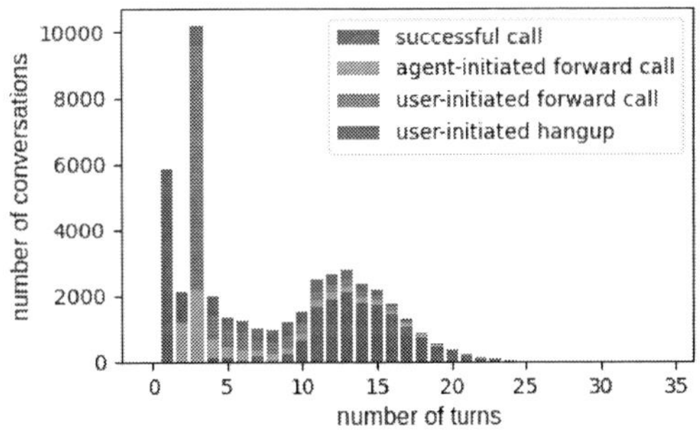

Figure 1: Distribution of the different types of phone calls over the number of turns on a sample of 45,385 conversations.

Given these considerations, we focus on user-initiated forward calls and hang-ups occurring late in the conversation. We will refer to these calls as to **LUHFs** (**L**ate **U**ser-initiated **H**ang-ups or **F**orward calls), a particular class of dialog breakdowns.

LUHFs are the types of calls that we aim to predict (positive examples). We consider as *late* conversations all the calls that reach at least the 8th turn. On the other hand, late successful calls are the negative examples of the dataset. In particular, we sample successful calls and then truncate the conversations at a random point (still, after the

Utterance	Intent	Entities
S: Are you a registered customer?	ask_if_current_client	
H: Uhm no	negate	
S: Can I book your service appointment under the phone number ending in <1234>?	confirm_phone_number	user_phone_suffix
H: Yeah that's correct	confirm	
S: What is the brand, model and year of your phone device?	new_user_profile_brand_model_year	
H: It's a <phonepink> why 100 <2022>	inform	brand_device, year
S: What is the model of phone device?	ask_device_model	
H: It is <y100>	inform	model_device
S: What is the battery health percentage of your phone device?	ask_for_battery_health	
H: <zero>	inform	numeric
S: What is your first name?	ask_first_name	ask_last_name
H: My name's <John>	inform	client_name
S: Great, what is your last name?	ask_last_name	
H: <Smith>	inform	client_name
S: What service does your phone device need?	ask_desired_service	
H: Uhm <battery replacement>	inform	type_of_repair

Table 2: Extract of a conversation between the system and a human. The entity values are enclosed by angular parentheses in the utterances.

"late"-call threshold). The user-initiated forward calls are also truncated from the point when the caller asks to be transferred. The ratio successful calls/LUHFs is 2:1. As a result, the dataset contains 13,524 calls (4,508 LUHFs and 9,016 not LUHFs).

Let us notice that the dataset contains noisy data because it is automatically annotated. Conversations may lead to a user-initiated forward, for example, even if there was no indication of user frustration. Similarly, a user may become irritated with the conversation but still decide to end the call. Moreover, it is worth noticing that the provided annotation is not at the utterance-level. Instead, a LUHF/not LUHF annotation refers to the overall conversation. In other words, if a conversation is a LUHF, we are not aware of at which point of the conversation a breakdown occurred. These elements make the predictions more challenging.

3.2 Dataset Features

The dialog system is composed of different modular components, including an NLU and an NLG component. The NLU provides annotations to the user's utterances, i.e. the *intent* and the *entities*, recognized by an intent classifier and a named-entity recognition system respectively. The NLG also provides the name of the *intent* and the *entities*, uttered by the system. The NLG intents are always different from the NLU intents. On the other hand, the NLG and NLU may have some entities in common.

3.3 Dataset Anonymization for Privacy Preservation

We anonymize the original data to protect the privacy of the original conversation content. In particular, we remove natural-language text and entity values. Keeping only the intent and entity annotations guarantees the privacy of the data.

We report an example of a fictitious conversation in Table 2, reporting the utterances exchanged between the system and a human. The detected entities are enclosed by angular parentheses in the utterances. We can notice that the caller releases sensitive information, such as the name and phone number. The entities and the intents are a synthetic way to represent the utterances, and therefore to substitute the utterances with these annotations is a valid way to proceed. One may argue that, in order to not lose much information, it could be possible to keep the text and remove only the entity values. This approach would work fine only with a perfect NLU that is able to recognize all the entities in the text. As we can see from Table 2, the entity `model_device` is not detected the first time. Moreover, the caller may reveal other types of sensitive information that an NLU is not supposed to detect. Since the NLU is prone to these errors and may not detect an entity in the text, it is indeed safer to remove all the textual information to preserve the privacy of the data.

# labels	# not LUHFs	9016
	# LUHFs	4508
	# LUHs	2477
	# LUFs	2765
# turns	min	8
	max	34
	avg	10
# NLG and NLU unique intents		91
# NLG and NLU unique entities		41

Table 3: BETOLD dataset statistics.

Table 3 reports the main dataset statistics. The resulting privacy-preserving dataset, named BETOLD (Breakdown Expectation for Task-Oriented Long Dialogues), is available at the following link: `https://github.com/telepathylabsai/BETOLD_dataset`.

4 An Attention-based Model for LUHF Detection

The task in BETOLD dataset is to classify if a conversation between a human and the system is a LUHF or not. In this setting, it is fundamental to keep track of what happened in the past, represented by the dialog history. We therefore investigate an attention-based architecture (Vaswani et al., 2017), that has proved to perform well in several dialog-related tasks (Qin et al., 2021; Colombo et al., 2020; Zhao and Kawahara, 2019; Hori et al., 2016), including dialog breakdown detection (Park et al., 2017).

4.1 Model Architecture

A conversation between a human and the system can be represented as a sequence x of n tuples, where each element of a tuple represents a different feature. Here, the features include the caller name (either NLG or NLU), the intents, and the entities. The sets of possible values (also called vocabularies) of each feature are represented by C, I, and E for the caller names, intents and entities respectively. The sequence x is then:

$$x = (c_1, i_1, e_1), (c_2, i_2, e_2), \dots, (c_n, i_n, e_n) \quad (1)$$

where (c_j, i_j, e_j) is a tuple composed of a caller name $c_j \in C$, an intent $i_j \in I$ and an entity set $e_j \in \mathcal{P}(E)$ and $j = 1, \dots, n$. We refer to the entities as *entity set*, because for each tuple, we can have zero, one or more entities. The vocabulary sets C, I and E have different dimensions, to which we add an *unknown* symbol for unseen elements and a *padding* symbol.

For each of these features, the model learns embedded representations of dimension m. These vector representations are then summed up, obtaining a m-dimensional vector, which is then passed through a positional encoding layer, to keep track of the order of each element of the sequence. The resulting sequence of m-dimensional vectors is used as input to the Transformer encoder. The Transformer encoder is a stack of t encoder layers of l dimensionality. The output sequence of the Transformer encoder is averaged and the resulting vector passes through a sequence of linear layers. Finally, we apply a sigmoid function to the last layer to get the predicted score (LUHF or not LUHF). We use a weighted Binary Cross Entropy (BCE) loss to optimize.

Figure 2 shows a sketch of the proposed architecture. Each type of feature is represented in a different color.

5 Experimental Setting

5.1 Text-only Baseline

Our goal is to demonstrate that a text-free model can achieve comparable performance to a text-based model. As a consequence, we consider the text-only model to be our baseline model. The available text is represented by the user and system utterances. We use Sentence-BERT (Reimers and Gurevych, 2019) to generate a contextualized sentence representation for each utterance.

We use the same type of architecture as the proposed model to ensure a fair comparison, except that the model's input is different, i.e. dense vector representations of text. We call this model `TEXT`.

5.2 Models

We compare the text-only baseline `TEXT` with different variants of the proposed model. To identify the single contribution of the entities and intents, we consider two variants of the model, namely `INT` and `ENT`, as the models that rely solely on intents or entities respectively. We then consider a model that combines all the features (intents, entities, and caller type (NLU or NLG)), referred to as `IEC`. The implementation of the models is available at

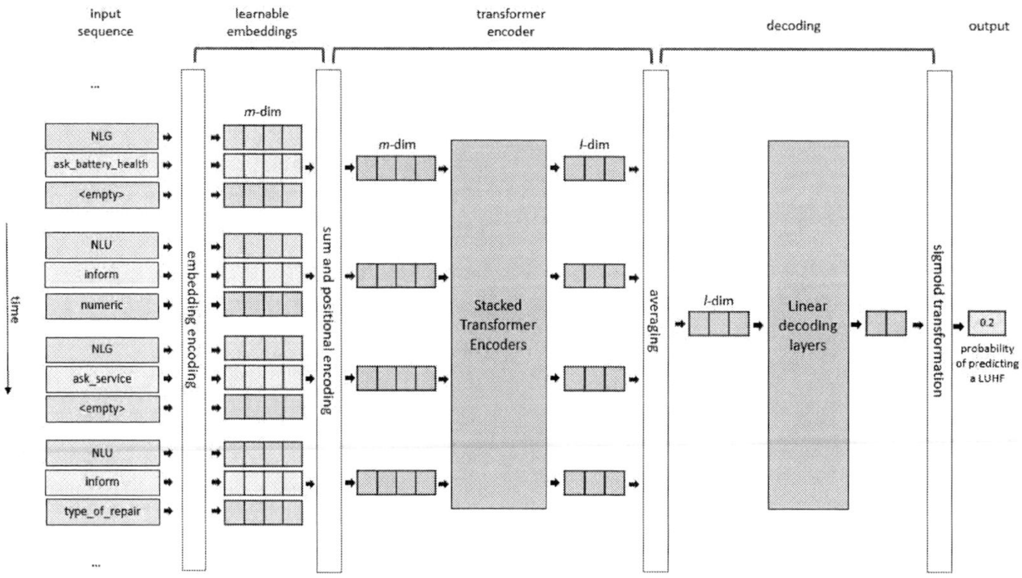

Figure 2: Sketch of the model architecture. To train the LUHF/not LUHF classifier multiple features are embedded and summed before a transformer encoder block followed by linear layers. The represented features are callers (orange, possible callers are "NLG" and "NLU"), intents (yellow, 91 intent names from NLU and NLG), and entities (blue, 41 entity names from NLU and NLG).

the following link: `https://github.com/telepathylabsai/dialog_breakdown_detection`.

5.3 Hyperparameter Setting

For running the experiments, we split the dataset into three parts: 80% for training, 10% for testing, and 10% for validation. We run all models for 50 epochs and then select the best model based on the validation set. We augment the training data by adding successful calls. In particular, we truncate the successful calls at random points and use them to expand the training data. We added 30% more successful calls to the overall training data. We do not perform data augmentation for the LUHFs because the LUHF annotation refers to the overall conversation and we have no hints about at which point in the conversation something went wrong.

We use grid search to determine the optimal hyperparameter configuration of the models. In particular, since we are more interested in the prediction of a LUHF rather than the prediction of a not LUHF, we select the optimal configuration based on the F1 score of the LUHF class. For the text-only model `TEXT`, we use the `all-MiniLM-L6-v2` pre-trained model to obtain the utterance representations.[1] Any document embedding model can be used to generate the utterances representations and feed the `TEXT` model. We run the `TEXT` model on the non-anonymized version of BETOLD, ensuring the same train/test/validation splits for a fair comparison. See Appendix A for further details on the hyperparameters.

6 Results

6.1 Quantitative Analysis

Table 4 reports the results of the models in terms of the F1 score for each class and the macro-averaged score. As a first remark, the models `ENT` and `INT` obtain a similar performance. This is probably due to the fact that some intents can be recognized by the entities of which they are composed. But since not all the intents are characterized by entities, the `ENT` model is not able to reach the same performance as the `INT` one.

Focusing on the `IEC` model, which combines the intents, entities, and caller type, we can notice that this model gets improved performance with re-

[1]See `https://huggingface.co/sentence-transformers/all-MiniLM-L6-v2`. In a preliminary investigation, we tried different pre-trained sentence embedding models made available by Hugging Face. Here, we report the results with the best performing model.

	LUHF F1	not LUHF F1	Macro avg F1
TEXT	0.798 ± 0.016	0.903 ± 0.005	0.850 ± 0.010
INT	0.727 ± 0.018	0.877 ± 0.002	0.802 ± 0.010
ENT	0.707 ± 0.018	0.867 ± 0.007	0.787 ± 0.011
IEC	0.744 ± 0.008	0.879 ± 0.003	0.812 ± 0.005

Table 4: Results of the considered models in terms of F1 score. We report the average and the deviation of 5 independent runs with the same hyperparameter configuration.

spect to the INT and ENT counterparts, as expected. IEC also obtains good performance if compared with the text-only baseline. It is worth noticing that the TEXT model is indeed a strong baseline: the intents and entity annotations provided by the dialog manager synthesize the meaning of an utterance, mapping them to a finite set of intents and entities. With this process, we inevitably lose some information about the dialog. Moreover, intent and entity annotations are prone to classification errors: the NLU may misclassify an intent or it may not detect an entity. Despite these difficulties, the IEC model can reach a comparable performance to the TEXT baseline, suggesting that it is possible to confidently identify a breakdown even without taking text into account.

6.2 Qualitative Analysis

In this section, we discuss some qualitative examples of the IEC model on the test set, one of a LUHF classification and one of a not LUHF misclassified as a LUHF.

Let us consider the conversation shown in Table 5. For each step of the conversation, we report the corresponding caller type (NLG or NLU), the intent, the entities, and the probability of identifying a LUHF. We filter out the first steps of the conversations due to space limitations. Let us recall that the LUHF annotation corresponds to the overall call. Therefore the model was not trained on each step of the conversation because there is no information about if a breakdown occurred at a given step. We will further discuss this issue in Section 7. Nevertheless, we can still compute the probability of identifying a LUHF at each step for a conversation, by generating a synthetic dataset composed of the same conversation but incrementally truncated.

Table 5 shows that the probability of detecting a LUHF increases as the conversation progresses. However, the probability often decreases after a user input, represented by an NLU annotation. We presume that this behavior happens because a user is less likely to hang up after replying and would wait until the next utterance before deciding to hang up. For example, at step 23, a user negates the proposed date of the system. This may be a signal of a breakdown and indeed the probability of a LUHF increases at step 24. The intent *time_asked_unavailable_propose_new* indicates an NLG intent where a time preference proposed by the user is unavailable, therefore the system proposes a new time. This can be an additional signal for a breakdown, which in fact increases the probability of detecting a LUHF.

In Table 6, we report an example of a not LUHF that has been classified as a LUHF at the final step of the conversation. As before, we eliminated the early steps of the call, where the conversation flowed nicely. At steps 13 and 16, the probability of predicting a LUHF increases, although there are no clear indications of a breakdown. It is worth noting that in the previous example the probability of a LUHF also increased after the intent *propose_date* (Table 5). Many LUHFs may happen in correspondence to this intent, therefore biasing the model to believe that this intent is an indication of a breakdown.

7 Limitations

As mentioned in Section 3.1, the labels in BETOLD are automatically assigned to each conversation. Therefore, it is possible that a conversation where everything goes smoothly but suddenly the user decides to hang up is classified as LUHF. Similarly, the user may decide to reach the end of the conversation even if they are extremely unsatisfied with the call. This case is not considered a dialog breakdown.

In addition to this issue, a LUHF annotation applies to the overall call and is not an indication of what happened during at each step of the conversation. A model that generalizes well should be able to predict whether a LUHF happened at each step of the call. The process of data augmentation described in Section 5.3 is an attempt to address this issue. This is, however, limited to not LUHF calls, given that we have no guarantees on when a breakdown happened in a conversation. Instead, we are quite confident that, if a call was successful, it was also successful in the previous steps.

Step	Caller	Intent	Entities	Probability of LUHF
9	NLG	ask_for_battery_health		0.002
10	NLU	inform	numeric	0.000
11	NLG	ask_first_name		0.109
12	NLU	inform	client_name	0.002
13	NLG	ask_last_name		0.296
14	NLU	inform	client_name	0.016
15	NLG	ask_desired_service		0.344
16	NLU	user_initial_request	type_of_repair	0.033
17	NLG	ask_additional_service		0.262
18	NLU	inconclusive		0.012
19	NLG	transportation_of_device	ask_to_schedule, ask_means_of_transportation	0.253
20	NLU	confirm		0.014
21	NLG	inform_schedule_inspection		0.012
22	NLG	propose_date	transportation_type_selection, available_slot_to_schedule	0.269
23	NLU	negate		0.033
24	NLG	ask_time_preference		0.378
25	NLU	user_proposed_date	time_range_indication	0.153
26	NLG	time_asked_unavailable_propose_new	transportation_type_selection, available_slot_to_schedule, user_request_start_time	0.922
27	NLU	negate		0.764
28	NLG	ask_time_preference		0.960

Table 5: Example of LUHF conversation correctly classified.

Figure 3 shows a density histogram of the probability by class of predicting a LUHF, averaged over all the conversation steps, for the test set conversations. As we can observe in the plot, the average probability of predicting a LUHF in a not LUHF call is low in general. We recall that we have more data available for the successful calls (the not LUHFs are two times more than the LUHFs and, in addition, we add 30% more successful calls through augmentation). Therefore, it is not surprising to see that the not LUHF distribution is more skewed towards to 0 than the LUHF distribution. Moreover, the results shown in the plot correspond to the average score across many steps of the conversation. A breakdown may happen very late in the conversation, thus resulting in an overall low average score. However, this is hard to determine through an automatic investigation and would require a manual inspection.

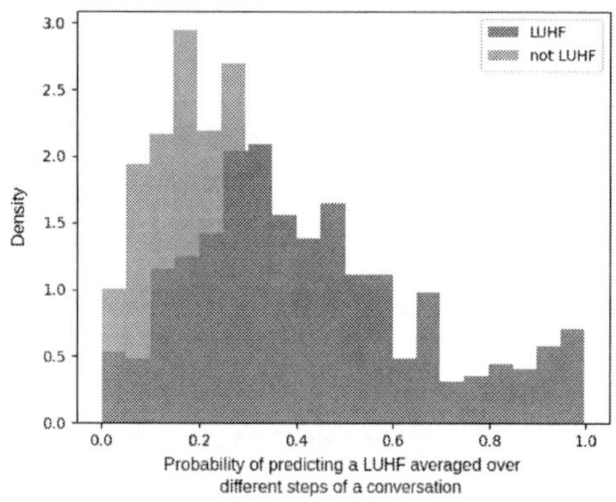

Figure 3: Histogram of the average probability of predicting a LUHF by class.

8 Conclusions

In this paper, we proposed a simple way to automatically generate a breakdown detection dataset in task-oriented dialogs, where the breakdown labels are extracted by user-initiated events. This dataset guarantees the privacy of the data by only keeping the annotations from NLU and NLG components. We proposed an attention-based model which uses these types of annotations. As a result, we demonstrated that a model does not necessarily require textual utterances to predict a breakdown; yet, it can benefit from the NLG and NLU intents and entities, automatically provided by a classical dialog system.

Step	Caller	Intent	Entities	Probability of LUHF
11	NLG	transportation_of_device	ask_means_of_transportation, ask_to_schedule	0.164
12	NLU	confirm		0.005
13	NLG	ask_time_preference		0.391
14	NLU	confirm		0.011
15	NLG	inform_schedule_inspection		0.005
16	NLG	propose_date	transportation_type_selection, available_slot_to_schedule	0.678

Table 6: Example of not LUHF conversation misclassified as a LUHF.

We also discussed some possible limitations of the model and the dataset, connected to the annotation schema. An automatic annotation, as it often happens, results in noisy data. However, we do believe that the proposed dataset is a promising starting point, which can save resources and could be further improved through manual annotations.

As highlighted by the qualitative analysis, it is worth further investigating the results to understand which elements play a role in the detection of a LUHF. The implementation of explainability methods can be an important tool in this context (Lundberg and Lee, 2017). Given the transformer-based architecture of our proposed model, current explainability tools (Kokhlikyan et al., 2020; Attanasio et al., 2022) can enrich our investigation of the role of each attention head in the breakdown prediction. For that, gradient-based methods can give an overview of the importance of individual features as well as of the interactions.

References

Giuseppe Attanasio, Eliana Pastor, Chiara Di Bonaventura, and Debora Nozza. 2022. ferret: a Framework for Benchmarking Explainers on Transformers. *arXiv preprint*.

Dennis Benner, Edona Elshan, Sofia Schöbel, and Andreas Janson. 2021. What do you mean? A Review on Recovery Strategies to Overcome Conversational Breakdowns of Conversational Agents. In *International Conference on Information Systems (ICIS)*.

Petter Bae Brandtzæg and Asbjørn Følstad. 2018. Chatbots: changing user needs and motivations. *Interactions*, 25(5):38–43.

Pierre Colombo, Emile Chapuis, Matteo Manica, Emmanuel Vignon, Giovanna Varni, and Chloe Clavel. 2020. Guiding attention in sequence-to-sequence models for dialogue act prediction. In *Proceedings of the AAAI Conference on Artificial Intelligence*, volume 34, pages 7594–7601.

Allen L. Gorin, Giuseppe Riccardi, and Jeremy H. Wright. 1997. How may I help you? *Speech Commun.*, 23(1-2):113–127.

Mariya Hendriksen, Artuur Leeuwenberg, and Marie-Francine Moens. 2021. LSTM for dialogue breakdown detection: exploration of different model types and word embeddings. In *Increasing Naturalness and Flexibility in Spoken Dialogue Interaction*, pages 443–453. Springer.

Ryuichiro Higashinaka, Kotaro Funakoshi, Masahiro Araki, Hiroshi Tsukahara, Yuka Kobayashi, and Masahiro Mizukami. 2015. Towards taxonomy of errors in chat-oriented dialogue systems. In *Proceedings of the 16th annual meeting of the special interest group on discourse and dialogue*, pages 87–95.

Ryuichiro Higashinaka, Kotaro Funakoshi, Yuka Kobayashi, and Michimasa Inaba. 2016. The dialogue breakdown detection challenge: Task description, datasets, and evaluation metrics. In *Proceedings of the Tenth International Conference on Language Resources and Evaluation (LREC'16)*, pages 3146–3150.

Takaaki Hori, Hai Wang, Chiori Hori, Shinji Watanabe, Bret Harsham, Jonathan Le Roux, John R Hershey, Yusuke Koji, Yi Jing, Zhaocheng Zhu, et al. 2016. Dialog state tracking with attention-based sequence-to-sequence learning. In *2016 IEEE Spoken Language Technology Workshop (SLT)*, pages 552–558. IEEE.

Minlie Huang, Xiaoyan Zhu, and Jianfeng Gao. 2020. Challenges in building intelligent open-domain dialog systems. . *ACM Transactions on Information Systems (TOIS)*, 38(3):1–32.

Sosuke Kato and Tetsuya Sakai. 2017. RSL17BD at DBDC3: computing utterance similarities based on term frequency and word embedding vectors. In *Proceedings of DSTC6.*, volume 34, pages 37–44.

Narine Kokhlikyan, Vivek Miglani, Miguel Martin, Edward Wang, Bilal Alsallakh, Jonathan Reynolds, Alexander Melnikov, Natalia Kliushkina, Carlos Araya, Siqi Yan, and Orion Reblitz-Richardson. 2020. Captum: A unified and generic model interpretability library for pytorch.

Seolhwa Lee, Dongyub Lee, Danial Hooshyar, Jaechoon Jo, and Heuiseok Lim. 2020. Integrating breakdown detection into dialogue systems to improve knowledge management: encoding temporal utterances with memory attention. *Information Technology and Management*, 21(1):51–59.

Scott M. Lundberg and Su-In Lee. 2017. A unified approach to interpreting model predictions. In *Advances in Neural Information Processing Systems 30: Annual Conference on Neural Information Processing Systems 2017, December 4-9, 2017, Long Beach, CA, USA*, pages 4765–4774.

Bilyana Martinovski and David Traum. 2003. Breakdown in human-machine interaction: the error is the clue. In *Proceedings of the ISCA tutorial and research workshop on Error handling in dialogue systems*, pages 11–16.

Kazuyuki Matsumoto, Manabu Sasayama, Minoru Yoshida, Kenji Kita, and Fuji Ren. 2022. Emotion analysis and dialogue breakdown detection in dialogue of chat systems based on deep neural networks. *Electronics*, 11(5).

Raveesh Meena, José Lopes, Gabriel Skantze, and Joakim Gustafson. 2015. Automatic detection of miscommunication in spoken dialogue systems. In *Proceedings of the 16th Annual Meeting of the Special Interest Group on Discourse and Dialogue*, pages 354–363.

Chanyoung Park, Kyungduk Kim, and Songkuk Kim. 2017. Attention-based dialog embedding for dialog breakdown detection. In *Proceedings of the dialog system technology challenges workshop (DSTC6)*.

Libo Qin, Zhouyang Li, Wanxiang Che, Minheng Ni, and Ting Liu. 2021. Co-GAT: A Co-Interactive Graph Attention Network for Joint Dialog Act Recognition and Sentiment Classification. In *Thirty-Fifth AAAI Conference on Artificial Intelligence, AAAI 2021*, pages 13709–13717. AAAI Press.

Nils Reimers and Iryna Gurevych. 2019. Sentence-bert: Sentence embeddings using siamese bert-networks. In *Proceedings of the 2019 Conference on Empirical Methods in Natural Language Processing and the 9th International Joint Conference on Natural Language Processing (EMNLP-IJCNLP)*, pages 3982–3992.

Alexander Schmitt, Benjamin Schatz, and Wolfgang Minker. 2011. Modeling and predicting quality in spoken human-computer interaction. In *Proceedings of the SIGDIAL 2011 Conference*, pages 173–184.

J Shin, Alireza Dirafzoon, and Aviral Anshu. 2019. Context-enriched attentive memory network with global and local encoding for dialogue breakdown detection. *Proceedings of the WOCHAT*.

Hiroaki Sugiyama. 2021. Dialogue breakdown detection using BERT with traditional dialogue features. In *Increasing Naturalness and Flexibility in Spoken Dialogue Interaction*, pages 419–427. Springer.

Ashish Vaswani, Noam Shazeer, Niki Parmar, Jakob Uszkoreit, Llion Jones, Aidan N Gomez, Łukasz Kaiser, and Illia Polosukhin. 2017. Attention is all you need. In *Advances in Neural Information Processing Systems 30: Annual Conference on Neural Information Processing Systems 2017*, pages 5998–6008.

Mattias Wahde and Marco Virgolin. 2022. Conversational agents: Theory and applications. *arXiv preprint*.

Marilyn A. Walker, Irene Langkilde, Jeremy H. Wright, Allen L. Gorin, and Diane J. Litman. 2000. Learning to predict problematic situations in a spoken dialogue system: Experiments with how may I help you ? In *6th Applied Natural Language Processing Conference, ANLP 2000, Seattle, Washington, USA, April 29 - May 4, 2000*, pages 210–217. ACL.

Chih-Hao Wang, Sosuke Kato, and Tetsuya Sakai. 2021. RSL19BD at DBDC4: ensemble of decision tree-based and LSTM-based models. In *Increasing Naturalness and Flexibility in Spoken Dialogue Interaction*, pages 429–441. Springer.

Jason D. Williams, Matthew Henderson, Antoine Raux, Blaise Thomson, Alan W. Black, and Deepak Ramachandran. 2014. The dialog state tracking challenge series. *AI Mag.*, 35(4):121–124.

Runhua Xu, Nathalie Baracaldo, and James Joshi. 2021. Privacy-preserving machine learning: Methods, challenges and directions. *arXiv preprint*.

Zheng Zhang, Ryuichi Takanobu, Qi Zhu, MinLie Huang, and XiaoYan Zhu. 2020. Recent advances and challenges in task-oriented dialog systems. *Science China Technological Sciences*, 63(10):2011–2027.

Tianyu Zhao and Tatsuya Kawahara. 2019. Joint dialog act segmentation and recognition in human conversations using attention to dialog context. *Computer Speech & Language*, 57:108–127.

A Hyperparameter Search

We report the hyperparameter space in Table 8. Table 7 shows the optimal hyperparameters selected after the grid search approach. We train the models for 15 epochs and select the best result based on the F1 score for the LUHF class on the validation set.

B Computing Infrastructure

We ran the experiments on a machine equipped with AMD® Ryzen 9 5900hx CPU, NVIDIA GeForce RTX 3060 GPU with CUDA v11.4, Driver Version 470.141.03 and 32GB RAM.

Parameter Description	Value
Embedded representations dimension l	400
Transformer Encoder embeddings dimension m	128
# layers of the Transformer Encoder t	3
# attention heads of the Transformer Encoder	16
Dropout ratio applied in the Transformer Encoder	0.01
Learning Rate	0.0001
Size of layers of decoding stage	(256, 32)
Optimizer	Adam
Number of epochs	15
BCE weight for not LUHFs	1.0
BCE weight for LUHFs	3.0

Table 7: Hyperparameters used for training the models.

Parameter Description	Value
Embedded representations dimension l	[256, 400, 800]
Transformer Encoder embeddings dimension m	[64, 128, 256]
# layers of the Transformer Encoder t	[1, 3, 5]
# attention heads of the Transformer Encoder	[4, 8, 16]
Dropout ratio applied in the Transformer Encoder	[0.01, 0.1, 0.5]
Learning Rate	[0.0001, 0.0005, 0.001]
Size of layers of decoding stage	[(256, 32), (256, 128, 32), (256, 64), (256, 128, 64), (256, 128, 64, 32)]
Optimizer	Adam
Number of epochs	50
BCE weight for not LUHFs	1.0
BCE weight for LUHFs	[1.0, 3.0, 5.0, 10.0]

Table 8: Hyperparameter space used for grid search.

Insurance Question Answering via Single-turn Dialogue Modeling

Seon-Ok Na and **Young-Min Kim** * and **Seung-Hwan Cho**
Department of Industrial Data Engineering
Hanyang University, Seoul, Republic of Korea
{nso94,yngmnkim,shcho95}@hanyang.ac.kr

Abstract

With great success in single-turn question answering (QA), conversational QA is currently receiving considerable attention. Several studies have been conducted on this topic from different perspectives. However, building a real-world conversational system remains a challenge. This study introduces our ongoing project, which uses Korean QA data to develop a dialogue system in the insurance domain. The goal is to construct a system that provides informative responses to general insurance questions. We present the current results of single-turn QA. A unique aspect of our approach is that we borrow the concepts of intent detection and slot filling from task-oriented dialogue systems. We present details of the data construction process and the experimental results on both learning tasks.

1 Introduction

Although there has been significant progress in single-turn question answering (QA), it cannot cover complex questions of realistic scenarios (Fu et al., 2020). Recently, multi-turn (conversational) QA has emerged as an alternative to address this problem by clarifying the questions via conversation (Qu et al., 2019a, 2020; Li et al., 2019; Reddy et al., 2019). Conversational QA is a category of dialogue systems which are divided into task-oriented, chitchat, and QA systems (Deriu et al., 2020; Zaib et al., 2021). However, QA is not always distinct from the other two categories.

In this study, we are interested in building a dialogue system in a restricted domain, insurance. The system aims to provide users with general descriptions of cancer insurance. We assumed the task is not pre-defined and should be specified from the data. A significant difficulty is that complete conversational data does not exist. Therefore, we needed to find other types of source data similar to the dialogues between users and experts on cancer insurance. The first is Q&A data from a Korean online QA service.

Although our goal is to construct a multi-turn dialogue system, this study covers only the single-turn QA corresponding to the target system's front part. The novelty of the present study is that we designed the system considering the further extension to multi-turns. Therefore, unlike the existing KB-based or neural QA systems, we borrow the concept of intent detection and slot filling from task-oriented dialogue systems (Gao et al., 2018).

The Transformer-based pre-trained models such as Bidirectional Encoder Representations from Transformers (BERT) achieved excellent performance for NLP tasks. BERT is one of the pioneers of the pre-trained language representation models (Devlin et al., 2018). Since it was proposed in 2018, a paradigm shift has taken place in the NLP domain. Most NLP tasks now are based on pre-trained language models. Meanwhile, there are also previous studies using directly BERT embeddings directly to express queries for conversational QA or FAQ retrieval (Qu et al., 2019b; Mass et al., 2020; Qu et al., 2020; Sakata et al., 2019). We use a Korean version of Electra (Clark et al., 2020), a variant of BERT, for intent detection and slot filling.

This study introduces intermediate results of our ongoing project on dialogue system construction in the insurance domain. We encountered many challenging situations from the first stage, data collection. We designed the system to be constructed using single-turn QA data but to finally serve as a multi-turn dialogue system. In the remainder of this paper, we describe the process of constructing training data for insurance QA in Section 2. Then the methods used for intent detection, slot filling, and the other approaches for the answer retrieval are presented in Section 3. Section 4 presents the experimental results for both learning tasks, including a quantitative analysis of the answer retrieval

*Corresponding author: Young-Min Kim

Proceedings of the 2nd Workshop on When Creative AI Meets Conversational AI (CAI2), COLING 2022, pages 35–41
October 12–17, 2022.

result. Then we conclude with some future works in Section 5.

2 Insurance Data for Question Answering

2.1 Data Collection and Preprocessing

Consumer counseling data in the insurance domain does not come to the public because of information privacy. Therefore, we collected single-turn Q&A data from an online QA service called Naver Knowledge iN (KiN)[1], which is part of the biggest Korean web portal, Naver. Login portal users can ask questions and the answerers voluntarily participate in the service. There are various subject sections in which tasks are allocated according to their nature. We scraped the Q&A pairs answered by 25 insurance experts in the insurance sector. The number of scraped Q&A pairs is 12,734.

For a realistic system, we limited our target to cancer insurance. We filtered out the pairs that did not include "cancer" in the title. The remaining data had three main issues for constructing a dialogue system. First, it is not conversational because Naver KiN consists of single-turn Q&A data that are inappropriate for dialogue systems. Second, both task-oriented and QA types of questions were mixed. Although the questions sought relevant information, some were relatively close to the task completion, such as recommendations or buying. Third, the intents and slots were not explicit. Though there are rough sub-categories of the questions, it is challenging to specify user intentions. Moreover, the primary entity types were unclear because the task was undefined. Considering all these issues, we began by defining the user intents and main tasks, unlike the general QA system. We then defined the appropriate slots to complete the task. This is also intended for further extension to multiple turns.

2.2 Topic Modeling

The user intentions in our data are not explicit, unlike typical task-oriented systems. Moreover, the questions are usually not represented clearly because general users do not know the insurance terminologies that precisely describe their situations. We also found that some sentences were literal questions, while the others provided information.

All of the above characteristics make defining intents challenging. Topic modeling can be an appropriate solution to address this problem. It identifies latent topics from a set of documents in an unsupervised manner. We applied the following LDA (Blei et al., 2003), on the question data to extract common themes of user questions.

Several preprocessing such as stopwords elimination and noun extraction have been applied before training the model. The number of topics was fixed to 30, considering perplexity, coherence, and manual validation of topic model results. We re-categorized the extracted topics as six different upper topics: *recommendation*, *specific cancers*, *money-related*, *special contracts*, *particular insurance companies*, and *insurance terminologies*.

Then we manually classified each question into one of the six topics. To facilitate the process, we distributed keywords to each topic that represent the topics well. The candidate keywords were high-rank words of topic modeling results. A question with several keywords of a particular topic can be classified as the topic. Finally, we had the Q&A pairs with the topic label. The pairs of two topics, *recommendation* and *particular insurance companies*, were eliminated because the answers related to these two topics can be too subjective. For convenience, we excluded samples with more than 200 syllables in the question. Finally, we ahd 2,295 Q&A pairs as source data.

2.3 User Intents and Main Task

The Q&A pairs with the topic label were the source data for the system construction. We preprocessed the questions to imitate multi-turn conversations. A question was first separated into sentences, and we supposed that each corresponded to an utterance. Each sentence was a data instance in terms of intent detection.

We manually annotated each sentence with a user intent label considering the pre-annotated topic. A user intent here means a detailed purpose of the utterance. Therefore, it is different from the higher-level user intention that can be interpreted as a task. The finally defined intent types are listed in Table 1. In addition to the 2,295 Q&A pairs, we added manually generated 892 pairs to handle the class imbalance and data insufficiency issues. As an utterance can be a question or an information-offering one, the intents were also classified into two different categories: *Request* and *Inform*.

The high-level categories of *Request* intents may be interpreted as tasks for the dialogue system. For

[1] https://kin.naver.com/

Table 1: Intent type definition

Intent type	Definition	Action Type	Count
Personal information	Provide personal information for consultation	Inform	503
Subscription information	Subscribed insurance policy	Inform	480
Emphasis	Emphasis user request	Inform	147
Insurance options required	Options added to insurance policies	Inform	197
Cancer diagnosis details	A history of cancer diagnosis	Inform	149
Approximate premium or claim	Premium or claim that cannot be categorized into the others	Request	576
Claim availability	Questions about claim availability	Request	189
Claim process	Queries the insurance claims payment process	Request	63
Claim	Questions about claim with a stated amount	Request	75
Duplicate coverage	Questions about duplicate coverage availability	Request	85
Premium	Questions about premium with a stated amount	Request	67
Non-payment	Payment of unpaid insurance premiums	Request	41
Considerations	Questions to consider when subscribing to insurance	Request	80
Subscribe	Insurance policy subscription request	Request	288
Terminology Meaning	Request explain on Terminology terms	Request	95
Termination	Request for termination of insurance	Request	62
Greeting	Greeting	Greeting	94

example, *Claim availability*, *Claim process*, and *Claim* can be classified into a high-level category, *Claim-related.* Although the high-level category does not correspond to a task to complete like task-oriented systems; it can serve to reduce the scope of the QA. In other words, we borrowed the concepts of "task" and "slot" from task-oriented systems, expecting they could contribute to the clarification of user requirements.

2.4 Slots

The slots necessary for filling can be defined using concrete examples. We assumed several hypothetical conversation scenarios because the source data did not include conversational situations. Several slots can be defined from these scenarios. Moreover, we examined the frequent nouns extracted from the source data to determine whether they could be used as slot values. Finally, we obtained 11 slots, as presented in Table 2.

2.5 KB for Answers

Once the system recognizes what the user asks, it returns an appropriate answer. To this end, we constructed a KB as an FAQ, apart from the source Q&A pairs. We preferred choosing an operator from the KB over the source data because the real solutions are diverse for the same questions. The KB was constructed using FAQs provided by nine insurance companies and included various techniques, from common insurance sense to insurance products. There were 817 FAQ pairs. We also constructed an insurance terminology dictionary using term lists provided by four insurance companies.

3 Methods

3.1 Intent Detection and Slot Filling

We used a Korean ELECTRA version for intent detection and slot filling. ELECTRA is an efficient model which modified Masked LM in BERT to achieve performance similar to BERT with a lower computing power. Multilingual versions are also available, but a language-specific model generally outputs a better result.

Intent detection is interpreted as a classification problem, and slot filling corresponds to a sequence labeling task. The two models are trained separately using the same pre-trained model learned using Korean Wikipedia data. The selected pre-trained model is *KoElectra-base_v3* developed by monologg[2]. The model has been fine-tuned for both tasks.

3.2 Sentence BERT for FAQ mapping

Even if we finished the construction of the KB and the training data, we had a critical issue with building a dialogue system. We did not know which questions in the source data were answerable by the FAQ in KB. In other words, we needed the mappings between the source and KB questions. This process was for making a golden standard. Therefore, manual mapping is ideal; however, it is time-consuming.

Sentence-BERT(SBERT) can be an effective labor-saving tool. SBERT is a derivative model of BERT and is mainly used to calculate sentence expressions (Reimers and Gurevych, 2019). It has

[2]https://github.com/monologg/KoELECTRA

Table 2: Slot definition and the examples

Slot	Definition	Example	Count
GENDER	User's gender	여성(woman)	127
INSURANT	Family relation of the insurant	아버지(father)	189
COMPANY	Insurance company name	삼성생명(Samsung Life Insurance)	117
PAYMENT	Costs paid by users, including premium	보험료(premium)	773
CANCER_TYPE	Cancer to be covered by insurance	위암(cancer of the stomach)	151
DISEASE_LOG	User's disease history	위암(cancer of the stomach)	679
JARGON	Insurance-specific terms	고지의무(duty to notify)	907
PLAM_NAME	Name of insurance policy	내인생플러스보험(My Life Plus Insurance)	51
BODY_PART	Body parts subject to disease	갑상선(Thyroid)	157
OPERATION_LOG	User's surgical history	갑상선 수술(thyroid surgery)	288
INSURANCE_TYPE	Types of insurance	실손보험(indemnity insurance)	1,555

a pooling layer that is added to the existing BERT and uses Siamese Network and Triplet Network architectures. SBERT provides better sentence embeddings, especially when computing sentence similarity. Therefore, we used a Korean version of SBERT to map the source and KB questions.

The mapping process is as follows: 1) compute the SBERT embeddings of the source and FAQ questions, 2) for each source question, find the three most similar FAQ questions using cosine similarity, 3) manually map the source question and a FAQ question if the questions are semantically similar.

Two annotators carried out the mapping for cross-validation. After the annotation, approximately half of the source questions were mapped to the FAQ questions Q.

3.3 Symbol replacement in slot filling data via dictionary mapping

Among the slots, *PLAN_NAME* is difficult to detect because of its low occurrence and high diversity in values. Moreover, the slot values usually consist of multiple words and have descriptive phrases. These characteristics make recognizing the slot challenging. Another problem is that the newly-coined plan names continuously occur.

To enhance the detection performance of the slot, we invented a simple but effective heuristic method. The method uses a dictionary of insurance product names. The dictionary was constructed using real plan names scraped from insurance company websites. In addition to the original training data for slot filling, we added sentences with the masked product names. The added sentences had product names identified by dictionary mapping and predefined special symbols replace the product names.

This method has three advantages. First, it is effective for the complex slot values, including words from other slots. Many existing plan names include the words signifying *INSURANCE_TYPE* or *COMPANY*. We could handle this issue by replacing the plan names with symbols. Second, it can contribute to solving the imbalanced dataset problem. This method showed similar effects to synonym substitution, one of the text data augmentation methods. As a result, the prediction performance was improved by 3-5% compared to the previous one. Third, post-processing was unnecessary, even though we use a dictionary as important external information. We got both the benefits of dictionary matching and language model at a time. In this way, we could enhance the recall value of *PLAN_NAME*. Figure 1 shows the sentence embedding architecture when applying our approach.

3.4 Answer Retrieval

There are two types of QA: Knowledge-based QA and IR-based QA (Jurafsky and Martin, 2009). The former requires a well-structured KB, whereas the latter the large quantities of texts. However, as our case does not apply to either, we take another approach similar to the FAQ retrieval. Even though the further goal of this study is a conversational dialogue system, we aim at a single-turn QA for now. Therefore, we propose a transitionary retrieval approach to select the most similar FAQ given a user question.

After manual FAQ mapping in Section 3.2, we got a set of source questions mapped to the most similar FAQs. Given a source question (utterance), the mapped FAQ can be the correct response that our QA system should return. We devised a simple but effective method to retrieve the most similar FAQ for a user utterance.

We used the detected slot values and the TF-IDF-based keywords in the proposed method to retrieve a proper FAQ. There were three different types of

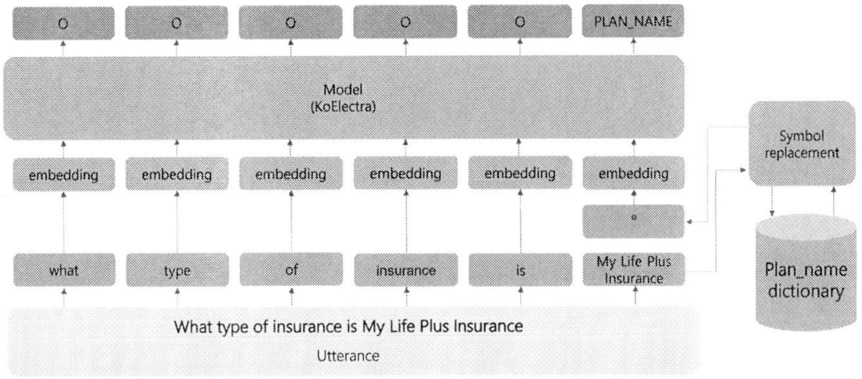

Figure 1: Sentence embeddings by symbol replacement via dictionary mapping

information to retrieve a good FAQ: 1) **set A** - the slot values and keywords detected from the user utterance; 2) **set B** - the slot values and keywords existing in the question part of each FAQ; and 3) **set C** - the slot values and keywords existing in the source questions that were mapped to each FAQ.

The overlapping score between sets A and B was computed for a given utterance and FAQ pair. A similar score was also computed for A and C. The weighted sum of these scores was the similarity score of the utterance-FAQ pair. We selected the FAQ that had the highest similarity score given an utterance.

4 Experiments

First, we present the experimental results for intent detection and slot filling. The former is a typical classification problem, and the latter can be interpreted as a sequence labeling task, as introduced in Section 3. KoElectra was for the training in both tasks. Second, we described the performance of answer retrieval from the FAQs. The weighted sum of the three scores was the similarity score of the utterance-FAQ pair: We selected the FAQ that had the highest similarity score given an utterance.

4.1 Intent detection and slot filling

Table 3 presents the experimental results of intent detection. The micro-averaged f1-score for 17 different intent types was 0.71. The result can be regarded as good given insufficient training data and many classes.

We had unsatisfactory results in the *Claim process* and *Premium* because some categories were similar to them, such as *Approximate premium or claim* and *Claim availability*. If the question was precisely for the insurance premium amount, the model classified the query into the class *Premium*. If not, the result was usually the class *Approximate premium or claim*. There are also a contextual similarity between the classes *Claim availability* and *Claim process*.

Table 3: Intent detection result

Intent type	precision	recall	f1-score
Personal information	0.83	0.79	0.81
Subscription information	0.84	0.83	0.83
Emphasis	0.97	0.89	0.93
Insurance options required	0.51	0.56	0.54
Cancer diagnosis details	0.59	0.79	0.68
Approximate premium or claim	0.58	0.57	0.58
Claim availability	0.67	0.83	0.74
Claim process	0.17	0.08	0.11
Claim	0.55	0.79	0.65
Duplicate coverage	0.88	0.68	0.77
Premium	0.30	0.25	0.27
Non-payment	0.75	0.50	0.60
Considerations	0.78	0.44	0.56
Subscribe	0.64	0.69	0.67
Terminology meaning	0.64	0.64	0.64
Termination	0.86	0.92	0.89
Greeting	1.00	0.92	0.96
macro average	0.68	0.66	0.66
micro average	0.71	0.71	0.71

For further verification, we show T-SNE visualization of 12th layer of the trained KoELECTRA in Figure 2. In the area marked with "1", there is a mix of the instances from two different classes, *Premium* (light green) and *Approximate premium or claim* (yellow). There is also another area, marked with "2", where the instances from *Claim availability* (dark green) *Claim process* (cyan). This result signifies that we further need to modify the category definition to separate well these confusable ones.

Table 4 lists the slot filling results. The micro-averaged f1-score is 0.95, which is a high value

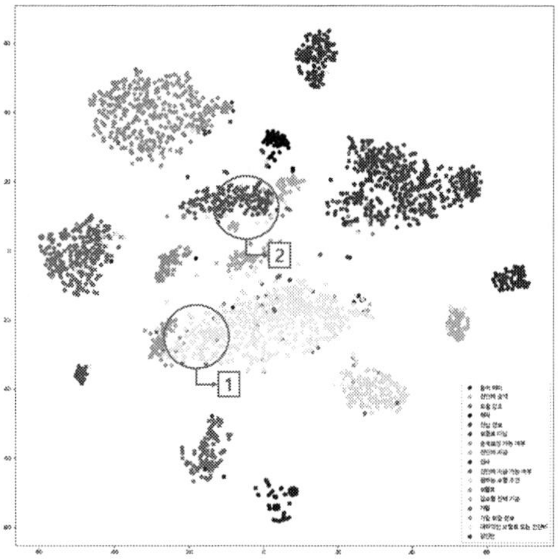

Figure 2: The T-SNE visualization of 12th layer of the trained KoELECTRA.

considering the number of slots. The worst f1-score, 0.58, is observed in the class *PLAN_NAME*, as we can easily guess from the discussion in Section 3.3. However, the result is enhanced compared to the other models trained without dictionary mapping, introduced in Section 3.3. Considering the class imbalance and insufficient training data, we found that the result was satisfactory.

Table 4: Slot filling result

Entity type	precision	recall	f1-score
GENDER	1.00	0.96	0.98
INSURANT	0.97	0.97	0.97
COMPANY	0.81	0.80	0.81
PAYMENT	0.93	0.99	0.96
CANCER_TYPE	0.93	0.83	0.88
DISEASE_LOG	0.89	0.93	0.91
JARGON	0.90	0.93	0.91
PLAN_NAME	0.46	0.76	0.58
BODY_PART	0.84	0.89	0.86
OPERATION_LOG	0.95	1.00	0.97
INSURANCE_TYPE	0.97	0.96	0.97
macro average	0.88	0.91	0.89
micro average	0.95	0.95	0.95

4.2 Answer Retrieval

We evaluated the FAQ retrieval results using the gold standard described in section 3.2. The accuracy was 70% on the test data. We also obtained acceptable results when generating random questions.

Table 5 presents two examples of the FAQ retrieval. Patterns exist in the mappings between the query and the FAQ. The two questions in the table show the representative ways. For the first query, the word "다시" (again) is the primary keyword enabling the mapping, which came from the set A introduced in Section 3.4. The second FAQ corresponds to a vast range of queries. Therefore, the FAQ is mapped to the appropriate queries especially conditioned on the slots and keywords of mapped source questions in the training data (set C in Section 3.4). Thus, the reason for mapping varies such that our strategy using the weighted sum score is proven effective for the answer retrieval.

Table 5: FAQ retrieval examples

	example
Query	이전에 위암으로 보장을 받았는데, 다시 암에 걸리면 보장 받을 수 있나요? (I had previously guaranteed stomach cancer. Can I get it if it recurs?)
1. Retrieved FAQ	보험금은 한번만 보장되나요? (Is this insurance guaranteed only once?)
2. Retrieved FAQ	암 진단 확정 시 보험금 청구서류 및 절차가 어떻게 되는 지 궁금합니다. (What are the procedures and documents required to claim insurance when diagnosed with cancer?)
3. Retrieved FAQ	지급기준이 어떻게 되나요? (What are the claim requirements for customer insurance?)
Query	오늘 보험에 가입했는데 언제부터 보장을 받을 수 있나요? (I bought insurance today, when I could get a guarantee?)
1. Retrieved FAQ	지급기준이 어떻게 되나요? (What are the claim requirements for customer insurance?)
2. Retrieved FAQ	가입하면 바로 보장을 받을 수 있나요? (Can I get a guarantee right away if I subscribe?)
3. Retrieved FAQ	보험금 청구를 하면 언제쯤 보험금이 지급되나요? (How long does it take to claim insurance?)

5 Conclusions

In this study, we built a single-turn dialogue system corresponding to the front part of our target system for the insurance domain. Our final goal is to construct a multi-turn dialogue system that can return informative counselors about insurance. For future scalability, the concept of intention detection and slot filling was borrowed, therefore, for this purpose, training data and KB was constructed on their own. We obtained an encouraging result for both tasks despite the limited quantity of the source. To enhance the performance of the slots with low occurrence and high-value diversity, we proposed a slot replacement method through dictionary mapping. The method also provided a good result. Future work first includes modifying category definitions and improving answer retrieval performance. Furthermore, we will re-design the system for the multi-turn dialogues. We expect the extracted intents and slot values to be effectively used for the multi-turn system.

Acknowledgement

This work was supported by two projects, AI-based ScienceOn User Behavior Prediction Technology, funded by KISTI (202200000001712) and Development of Next Generation Artificial Intelligence Assistant System Technology, funded by AIITONE (202200000000124).

References

David M. Blei, Andrew Y. Ng, Michael I. Jordan, and John Lafferty. 2003. Latent dirichlet allocation. *Journal of Machine Learning Research*, 3:2003.

Kevin Clark, Minh-Thang Luong, Quoc V. Le, and Christopher D. Manning. 2020. ELECTRA: pre-training text encoders as discriminators rather than generators. *CoRR*, abs/2003.10555.

Jan Deriu, Alvaro Rodrigo, Arantxa Otegi, Guillermo Echegoyen, Sophie Rosset, Eneko Agirre, and Mark Cieliebak. 2020. Survey on evaluation methods for dialogue systems. *Artificial Intelligence Review*.

Jacob Devlin, Ming-Wei Chang, Kenton Lee, and Kristina Toutanova. 2018. Bert: Pre-training of deep bidirectional transformers for language understanding. *arXiv preprint arXiv:1810.04805*.

Bin Fu, Yunqi Qiu, Chengguang Tang, Yang Li, Haiyang Yu, and Jian Sun. 2020. A survey on complex question answering over knowledge base: Recent advances and challenges. *CoRR*, abs/2007.13069.

Jianfeng Gao, Michel Galley, and Lihong Li. 2018. Neural approaches to conversational AI. In *Proceedings of the 56th Annual Meeting of the Association for Computational Linguistics: Tutorial Abstracts*, pages 2–7.

Dan Jurafsky and James H. Martin. 2009. *Speech and language processing: an introduction to natural language processing, computational linguistics, and speech recognition, 2nd Edition*. Prentice Hall series in artificial intelligence. Prentice Hall, Pearson Education International.

Xiaoya Li, Fan Yin, Zijun Sun, Xiayu Li, Arianna Yuan, Duo Chai, Mingxin Zhou, and Jiwei Li. 2019. Entity-relation extraction as multi-turn question answering. *CoRR*, abs/1905.05529.

Yosi Mass, Boaz Carmeli, Haggai Roitman, and David Konopnicki. 2020. Unsupervised FAQ retrieval with question generation and BERT. In *Proceedings of the 58th Annual Meeting of the Association for Computational Linguistics*, pages 807–812, Online. Association for Computational Linguistics.

Chen Qu, Liu Yang, Cen Chen, Minghui Qiu, W. Bruce Croft, and Mohit Iyyer. 2020. Open-retrieval conversational question answering. In *Proceedings of the 43rd International ACM SIGIR Conference on Research and Development in Information Retrieval*, SIGIR '20, page 539–548, New York, NY, USA. Association for Computing Machinery.

Chen Qu, Liu Yang, W. Bruce Croft, Yongfeng Zhang, Johanne R. Trippas, and Minghui Qiu. 2019a. User intent prediction in information-seeking conversations. In *Proceedings of the 2019 Conference on Human Information Interaction and Retrieval*, CHIIR '19, page 25–33, New York, NY, USA. Association for Computing Machinery.

Chen Qu, Liu Yang, Minghui Qiu, W. Bruce Croft, Yongfeng Zhang, and Mohit Iyyer. 2019b. Bert with history answer embedding for conversational question answering. In *Proceedings of the 42nd International ACM SIGIR Conference on Research and Development in Information Retrieval*, SIGIR'19, page 1133–1136, New York, NY, USA. Association for Computing Machinery.

Siva Reddy, Danqi Chen, and Christopher D. Manning. 2019. CoQA: A Conversational Question Answering Challenge. *Transactions of the Association for Computational Linguistics*, 7:249–266.

Nils Reimers and Iryna Gurevych. 2019. Sentence-BERT: Sentence embeddings using Siamese BERT-networks. In *Proceedings of the 2019 Conference on Empirical Methods in Natural Language Processing and the 9th International Joint Conference on Natural Language Processing (EMNLP-IJCNLP)*, pages 3982–3992, Hong Kong, China. Association for Computational Linguistics.

Wataru Sakata, Tomohide Shibata, Ribeka Tanaka, and Sadao Kurohashi. 2019. Faq retrieval using query-question similarity and bert-based query-answer relevance. In *Proceedings of the 42nd International ACM SIGIR Conference on Research and Development in Information Retrieval*, SIGIR'19, page 1113–1116, New York, NY, USA. Association for Computing Machinery.

Munazza Zaib, Wei Emma Zhang, Quan Z. Sheng, Adnan Mahmood, and Yang Zhang. 2021. Conversational question answering: A survey. *CoRR*, abs/2106.00874.

Can We Train a Language Model Inside an End-to-End ASR Model? - Investigating Effective Implicit Language Modeling

Zhuo Gong[1], Daisuke Saito[1], Sheng Li[2], Hisashi Kawai[2], and Minematsu Nobuaki[1]
[1]The University of Tokyo, Tokyo, Japan
[2]National Institute of Information and Communications Technology, Kyoto, Japan
gongzhuo@gavo.t.u-tokyo.ac.jp

Abstract

Language models (LM) have played crucial roles in automatic speech recognition (ASR) to enhance end-to-end (E2E) ASR systems' performance. There are two categories of approaches: finding better ways to integrate LMs into ASR systems and adapting on LMs to the task domain. This article will start with a reflection of interpolationbased integration methods of E2E ASR's scores and LM's scores. Then we will focus on LM augmentation approaches based on the noisy channel model, which is intrigued by insights obtained from the above reflection. The experiments show that we can enhance an ASR E2E model based on encoder-decoder architecture by pre-training the decoder with text data. This implies the decoder of an E2E model can be treated as an LM and reveals the possibility of enhancing the E2E model without an external LM. Based on those ideas, we proposed the implicit language model canceling method and then did more discussion about the decoder part of an E2E ASR model. The experimental results on the TED-LIUM2 dataset show that our approach achieves a 3.4% relative WER reduction compared with the baseline system, and more analytic experiments provide concrete experimental supports for our assumption.

1 Introduction

In the 1980s, a significant step was achieved by introducing the acoustic model (AM) and language model (LM) into ASR framework. From that time, the methodology of ASR shifted from the more intuitive template-based approach (a straightforward pattern recognition paradigm) towards a more rigorous statistical modeling framework (Juang and Rabiner, 2005). Moreover, those two concepts of AM and LM became the foundation of ASR that we are familiar with nowadays. Relying solely on acoustic observations proved to be insufficient to achieve human-like performance.

With the rapid development of deep learning techniques, many powerful neural network-based systems were invented in the new century. Among them, various end-to-end (E2E) systems become prevail (Battenberg et al., 2017; Chan et al., 2016; Kim et al., 2017; Watanabe et al., 2018; Vaswani et al., 2017), which are benefited from sufficient computing power and data sets. From this stage, E2E ASR becomes the mainstream of modern ASR techniques. We have emphasized the importance of LMs in ASR, but how an independent LM can be utilized in an E2E system? The answers are LM integration, and LM adaptation (Zhao et al., 2019; Shan et al., 2019; Sriram et al., 2018). LM integration increases accuracies of E2E ASR systems in practical indeed. However, intuitively, if an E2E ASR model is powerful enough, there is no need for an extra LM. So, the question becomes how an LM can benefit an E2E ASR system. To be more specific, we need to figure out what happens when we try to integrate the E2E ASR model with an LM and how to adapt an LM to an ASR domain. Furthermore, can we reveal the capability of language modeling in an E2E ASR model?

In this paper, we try to answer those questions theoretically and experimentally. Firstly, we analyzed shallow fusion of LM integration mathematically using LM adaptation framework (McDermott et al., 2019). Then, we proposed an implicit LM canceling method to fully control the language modeling functionality of an E2E ASR system. Finally, we discussed the feasibility that a decoder of an E2E ASR model could be treated as an LM by experiments. To the best of our knowledge, we are the first to analyze the language modeling functionality of the decoder part in an E2E ASR model.

The rest of this paper is structured as follows. Section 2 discusses the most common LM integration approach (shallow fusion) to explore its essence from the perspective of probability models.

Proceedings of the 2nd Workshop on When Creative AI Meets Conversational AI (CAI2), COLING 2022, pages 42–47
October 12–17, 2022.

Then we try to figure out a way to compose LM integration and LM adaptation tasks into a single method in Section 3 and 4. In Section 5, we analyze the result and reveal crucial insights about a decoder's characteristics in an E2E ASR system from several experiments. We conclude the paper in Section 6.

2 Related Work

2.1 LM Integration

In conventional ASR systems, whether or not based on deep learning, an LM is an essential part of the whole system. While in E2E models, an LM is not necessary since they can decode the intermediate representations of input features into a word sequence independently. For an E2E model, it is still beneficial to introduce an LM into the model. an LM is helpful for introducing extra corpora information. The main LM integration approaches in the previous work (Zhao et al., 2019; Shan et al., 2019; Sriram et al., 2018) are referred to as shallow, deep, and cold fusions. In the following section, we focus on investigating the details of shallow fusion.

In Eq. 1 of shallow fusion, $s(y|x)$ is the final score of output tokens based on input features x. The $\beta Penalty(|y|)$ is a penalty item, and it is a function of the output sequence length $|y|$ aiming at suppressing longer candidates. Since a longer sequence tend to produce more meaningless words, such as ah, em, its length should be suppressed. Moreover, α, β are hyper-parameters weighted to determine each item's importance in this equation.

$$\begin{aligned} s(y|x) = &\log(P_{E2E}(y|x)) \\ &+ \alpha \log(P_{LM}(y)) + \beta Penalty(|y|) \end{aligned} \tag{1}$$

where $P_{E2E}(y|x)$ and $P_{LM}(y)$ represent the conditional probabilities of a specific output sequence given input features to an E2E ASR model and an LM.

2.2 LM Adaptation

LM integration is just the first step to introduce LMs into ASR framework. To make an LM fit into a speech domain, we need to introduce LM adaptation. Then, we show how this method can be applied to LM integration analysis.

In previous work (McDermott et al., 2019), the density ratio approach is proposed as a transfer learning method based on Bayes' rule. This previous work studied LM representations in an E2E model. Moreover, this approach makes the following assumptions:

Table 1: List of key variables and their descriptions.

Variable	Description
$P_\phi(W,X)$	The source domain ϕ has some true joint distribution $P_\phi(W,X)$ over text (W) and audio (X)
$P_\tau(W,X)$	The target domain τ has another true joint distribution $P_\tau(W,X)$
$P_\phi(W\|X)$	A source domain E2E model (e.g., RNN-T (Battenberg et al., 2017)) captures $P_\phi(W\|X)$ reasonably well
$P_\phi(W)$ and $P_\tau(W)$	Separately trained LMs (e.g., RNN-LMs) capture $P_\phi(W)$ and $P_\tau(W)$ reasonably well
$p_\phi(X\|W)$ and $p_\tau(X\|W)$	$p_\phi(X\|W)$ as an acoustic model is roughly equal to $p_\tau(X\|W)$, i.e. the two domains are acoustically consistent

According to Bayes's rule, we have:

$$p_\phi(X|W) = p_\phi(X)P_\phi(W|X)/P_\phi(W) \tag{2}$$

Similarly, for the target domain:

$$p_\tau(X|W) = p_\tau(X)P_\tau(W|X)/P_\tau(W) \tag{3}$$

Since these two acoustic models roughly are the same:

$$\hat{P}_\tau(W|X) = k(X)\frac{P_\tau(W)}{P_\phi(W)}P_\phi(W|X) \tag{4}$$

With $k(X) = p_\phi(X)/p_\tau(X)$ shared by all hypotheses W, and density ratio method is named after the ratio $P_\tau(W)/P_\phi(W)$. Based on Eq. 4 we can give the score function of decoding process:

$$\begin{aligned} Score(W|X) = &\log P_\phi(W|X) + \lambda_\tau \log P_\tau(W) \\ &-\lambda_\phi \log P_\phi(W) + \beta \end{aligned} \tag{5}$$

where $Score(W|X)$ is our decoding logits score during beam search.

3 Implicit LM Canceling Method

Inspired by the density ratio approach, we propose to restructure the shallow fusion of Eq.1 in a more general way:

$$
\begin{aligned}
P_{rescoring}(W|X) &= \beta P_{E2E}(W|X)^{1-\lambda} P_{LM}(W)^{\lambda} \\
&= \beta \left(\frac{P_{E2E}(X|W) P_{E2E}(W)}{P_{E2E}(X)} \right)^{1-\lambda} P_{LM}(W)^{\lambda} \\
&= \beta \left(\frac{P_{E2E}(X|W) P_{E2E}(W) P_{LM}(W)^{\lambda/1-\lambda}}{P_{E2E}(X)} \right)^{1-\lambda}
\end{aligned}
$$

where $P_{rescoring}(W|X)$ is the score for a word sequence W given an observation X. $P_{E2E}(W|X)$ stands for our E2E model which gives the probability score of a word sequence given an observation X, and $P_{LM}(W)$ stands for an independent LM. $P_{E2E}(X|W)$ stands for an implicit pronunciation model inside the E2E model, while $P_{E2E}(W)$ represents the implicit LM inside the E2E model which we focus on. Since $P_{E2E}(X)$ is same for different word sequence candidate, this term should be omitted during scoring.

Then we have a probability score,

$$
\begin{aligned}
\exp(score(W|X)) = \\
P_{E2E}(X|W) P_{E2E}(W) P_{LM}(W)^{\hat{\lambda}},
\end{aligned} \tag{6}
$$

where $\hat{\lambda} = \lambda/1 - \lambda$

As we can see from Eq.6, the LM of an ASR system including an E2E model and an actual LM is $P_{E2E}(W) P_{LM}(W)^{\hat{\lambda}}$. That means by shallow fusion we can modify the final LM during rescoring. Moreover, it gives us the ability to change the implicit LM in an E2E model.

$$
\begin{aligned}
P(W|X) &= P_{E2E}(W|X) P_{LM}(W) / P_{E2E}(W) \\
&= \left(\frac{P_{E2E}(X|W) P_{E2E}(W)}{P_{E2E}(X)} \right) \frac{P_{LM}(W)}{P_{E2E}(W)} \\
&= \frac{P_{E2E}(X|W) P_{LM}(W)}{P_{E2E}(X)}
\end{aligned} \tag{7}
$$

where $P(W|X)$ is the probability model of the whole E2E ASR system which includes an E2E ASR model and an LM.

It should be noticed that we have no direct control (modify this model) over this implicit LM (as the probability density function $P_{E2E}(W)$) during decoding. One way to take control of the final LM is to cancel the E2E model's implicit LM and replace it with our external LM. This can be achieved by Eq.7. Just like what has been done in the density ratio approach, we train an E2E ASR model and a LM on audio and transcripts of the source domain speech corpus, and then another LM is pre-trained on extra gigantic corpora and fine-tuned on source domain text to approximate the true distribution of source domain. During decoding, the score function is Eq.8.

$$
\begin{aligned}
score(W|X) &= \log P_{E2E}(W|X) \\
&+ \log P_{LM}(W) - \log P_{E2E}(W)
\end{aligned} \tag{8}
$$

where $score(W|X)$ is the score for beam searching

We propose it as implicit LM canceling method. This kind of approach has no requirements for the E2E model (e.g., RNN-T in density ratio approach) and does not require hyper-parameters to tune the importance of two LMs. Thus, we can build an experimental ASR system based on the state-of-the-art transformer-encoder decoder model plus CTC loss (Kim et al., 2017) function in Fig. 1. The detailed settings can be found in Section 5.2.

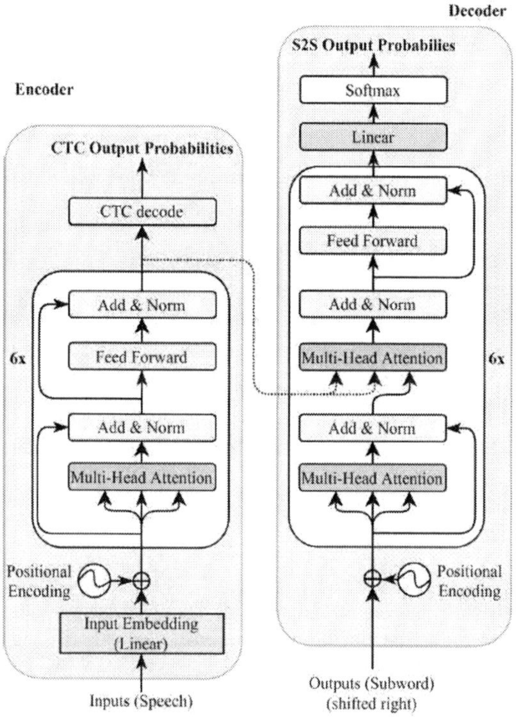

Figure 1: Transformer-based E2E ASR model jointly trained with CTC loss.

4 The Implicit LM of An E2E ASR System

We can check the assumption that the decoder of an E2E model can be treated as an LM from two aspects:

1. Is there a structure supporting the function of an LM in the E2E model?

2. Does it behave like an LM?

The decoder of this E2E model should potentially be an LM because it is an auto-regression model, just like a normal language model, which receives a token sequence and outputs the next token. It has transformer layers for memorizing information from the training set. And from Fig. 1 the multi-head attention layers which receive a word sequence and hidden states from the encoder are built relatively independent. So, we can assume the layers which did not receive hidden states directly from the encoder would be dominated by outputs (subword). Those characteristics above fulfill the first aspect. We can check the second statement by sampling token sequences in an auto-regression manner or calculate its perplexity about an LM's behaviors. Moreover, the above clarification leads to our new proposal: the decoder of an E2E model can be treated as an LM and be pre-trained on text data before E2E training to improve the E2E model. We will validate this in the following experiments.

5 Experiments

5.1 Task Descriptions

The experiments contain two parts: to validate our LM canceling method's performance and test a decoder's potential as an LM with more experiments.

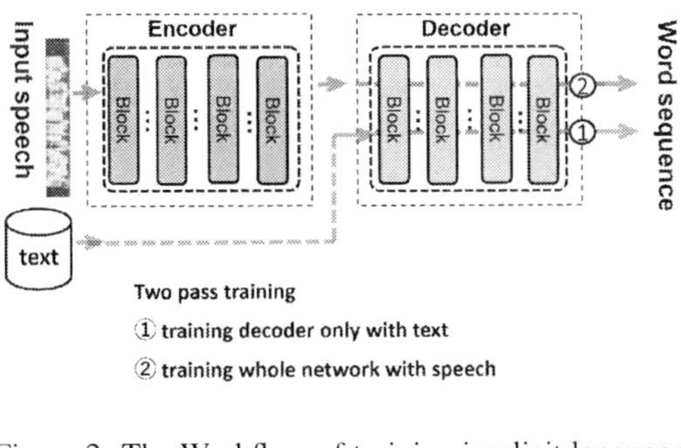

Figure 2: The Workflow of training implicit language model for E2E ASR model.

1. The first part is the same as a standard shallow fusion method. We calculate output logits of three models and apply Eq.7 during beam searching in the testing stage.

2. The second part in Fig. 2 is to train a decoder in an E2E ASR model as an LM. We implement this idea in a straightforward way. We set the intermediate vectors from the encoder to zeros and feed the decoder text corpus to output embedding in Fig. 1 just as if we are training a norm LM while completely omit the encoder. And then, several different experiments are conducted based on a decoder we trained in this manner. The decoders' perplexities and word error rate (WER) of the E2E ASR model with a different decoder are calculated as results.

5.2 Experimental Settings

We adopt a Transformer-based ASR system comprised of 6 encoder blocks and 6 decoder blocks with the feed-forward inner dimension of 2048, the model dimension of 256, and the attention head number 4, which are unchanged in all experiments. The input features were 240-dimensional log Mel-filterbank energy features (80-dim static, $+\Delta$, and $+\Delta\Delta$). The feature is extracted with a 10-ms frameshift of a 25-ms window. Each feature was mean- and variance-normalized per speaker, and every four frames were spliced (three left, one current, and zero right). The low and high cutoff frequencies were set to 20 Hz and 8,000 Hz, respectively. Speed perturbation was not used in the fine-tuning stage. We then subsampled the input features every three frames. The model was jointly trained with CTC (weight $\alpha = 0.2$). The "noam" optimizer was used with 25,000 warmup steps and an initial learning rate of 5. The model was trained with ESPnet toolkit (Watanabe et al., 2018) using batch-size 32 for 30 epochs on an 11-GB GTX1080 TI GPU.

The experiment is conducted on TED-LIUM2 (Rousseau et al., 2012), and the LMs are trained on text data offered by this corpus. Moreover, the LMs are four-layer transformer models.

5.3 Results and Discussions

The performances of the proposed LM canceling method are shown in Table 2 (+Transcripts LM means shallow fusion of the baseline model and

Table 2: Word Error Rate (WER) Results of E2E ASR with different LM settings

E2E baseline	+Transcripts LM (A)	+Text LM (B)	-A+B
11.7	11.6	10.5	11.3

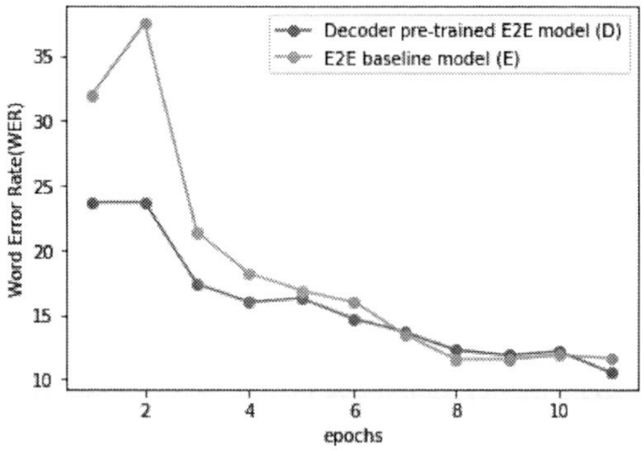

Figure 3: WER of decoder pretrained E2E model and E2E model trained from scratch.

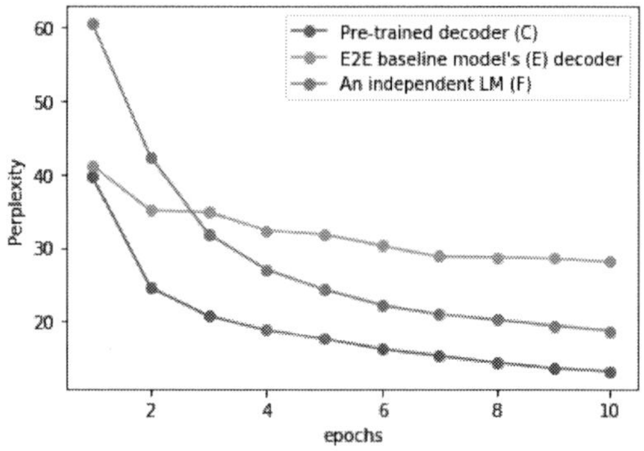

Figure 4: Perplexity of the decoder trained on transcripts, the E2E baseline model trained on paired audio and transcripts and an independent LM trained on transcripts.

an LM trained on transcripts from the baseline corpus; +Text LM means shallow fusion of baseline model and an LM trained on extra text corpus; -A+B means applying the method in Eq.8). We have to admit that results are not good as expected. One main reason is that we have made a strong assumption that the implicit LM $P_{E2E}(W)$ of an E2E model can be represented by an independent explicit LM. In the following section, we investigate why this assumption works not well.

To check the potential that a decoder can be treated as an LM further, we did more analytic experiments. We pre-trained the decoder (C) by feeding it transcripts from the source domain and set the hidden states to be zero vectors. Those hidden states are supposed to be passed from the

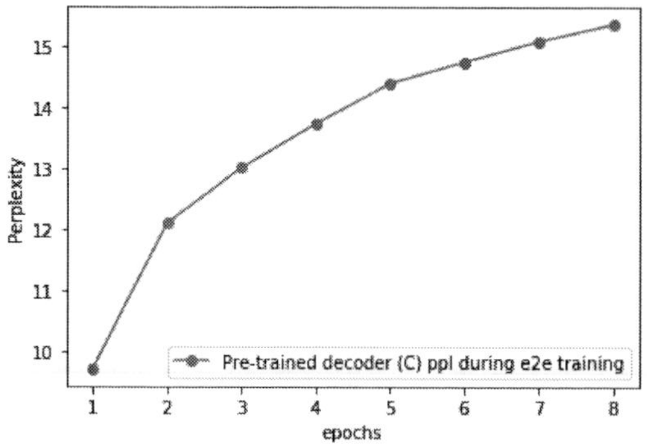

Figure 5: Perplexity of pre-trained E2E model during E2E training.

encoder to the decoder of the same E2E model. This method can ensure that no acoustic related weights will change during training of the decoder. After this decoder pre-training process, the E2E model (D) with the pre-trained decoder will be trained in the speech corpus. A baseline model (E) of the same structure as the previous one will be trained from scratch.

Several experiments are also conducted on the corpus TED-LIUM2, and all the LM training (including an independent LM (F) and the decoder (D)) are done on transcripts data of the speech corpus. All the E2E models are built on the same structure of transformer-based sequence-to-sequence model.

The results in Fig. 3 show that pre-training the decoder (C) as a language model does improve the performance of this E2E model (D). Fig. 4 shows the perplexity results for the decoder (C) and the LM (F) trained on transcripts and the E2E model (E) trained on the same transcripts with paired audio data.

As we can see in Fig. 4, the decoder's (C) perplexity effectively decreased during training and even decreased more rapidly than the LM (F), which may be related to more layers in the decoder. This can prove that the decoder (C) can be trained like an LM effectively. Moreover, the perplexity of the E2E model (E) trained from scratch decreased slowly. This phenomenon can explain why the implicit LM in the E2E model (in Table 2) should not be canceled by an external LM (A) trained even on the same transcripts. Because the LM performances of them are not even close. Fig. 5 gives the perplexity tendency of the decoder (C) in E2E training shown in Fig. 3.

The most interesting observation from it is that even the whole E2E model (D) becomes more accurate during training, but the decoder (C) part of it becomes worse as an LM, which implies the E2E training may harm the implicitly language modeling in the decoder (C). This phenomenon alerts all of the developers working on E2E models, and we will make an in-depth investigation to cope with it.

6 Conclusions

This article reflected why we introduced LMs into E2E ASR systems and discussed how LM integration benefits an E2E ASR system by generalizing shallow fusion by probability density function inspired by LM adaptation in ASR. In the general version of shallow fusion, insights about whether there is an implicit LM and how to modify it are obtained. This work reveals the decoder's potential to be trained and improve E2E models by training the decoder independently without external LMs. Moreover, we proposed the implicit LM canceling method. In the ordinary design of this transformer-based system, the decoder needs hidden states from an encoder, but we set these hidden states to zeros vectors to avoid acoustic feature-related weights changing in the decoder during pre-training. In the future, we will find a more sophisticated way to pre-train the decoder, alter the structure, modify the loss function, or change the training schedule. Moreover, we will try to figure out a way to suppress the degeneration phenomenon of the decoder's LM function (C) during E2E training.

In the next step, we plan to find a more sophisticated way to pre-train the decoder, alter the structure, modify the loss function, as well as change the training schedule. Moreover, we will try to figure out a way to suppress the degeneration phenomenon of the decoder's LM function (C) during E2E training.

References

Eric Battenberg, Jitong Chen, Rewon Child, Adam Coates, Yashesh Gaur Yi Li, Hairong Liu, Sanjeev Satheesh, Anuroop Sriram, and Zhenyao Zhu. 2017. Exploring neural transducers for end-to-end speech recognition. *2017 IEEE Automatic Speech Recognition and Understanding Workshop (ASRU)*, pages 206–213.

William Chan, Navdeep Jaitly, Quoc V. Le, and Oriol Vinyals. 2016. Listen, attend and spell: A neural network for large vocabulary conversational speech recognition. *2016 IEEE International Conference on Acoustics, Speech and Signal Processing (ICASSP)*, pages 4960–4964.

Biing-Hwang Juang and Lawrence R Rabiner. 2005. Automatic speech recognition–a brief history of the technology development. *Georgia Institute of Technology. Atlanta Rutgers University and the University of California. Santa Barbara*, 1:67.

Suyoun Kim, Takaaki Hori, and Shinji Watanabe. 2017. Joint ctc-attention based end-to-end speech recognition using multi-task learning. *2017 IEEE International Conference on Acoustics, Speech and Signal Processing (ICASSP)*, pages 4835–4839.

Erik McDermott, Hasim Sak, and Ehsan Variani. 2019. A density ratio approach to language model fusion in end-to-end automatic speech recognition. *2019 IEEE Automatic Speech Recognition and Understanding Workshop (ASRU)*, pages 434–441.

Anthony Rousseau, Paul Deléglise, and Y. Estève. 2012. Ted-lium: an automatic speech recognition dedicated corpus. In *LREC*.

Changhao Shan, Chao Weng, Guangsen Wang, Dan Su, Min Luo, Dong Yu, and Lei Xie. 2019. Component fusion: Learning replaceable language model component for end-to-end speech recognition system. *ICASSP 2019 - 2019 IEEE International Conference on Acoustics, Speech and Signal Processing (ICASSP)*, pages 5361–5635.

Anuroop Sriram, Heewoo Jun, Sanjeev Satheesh, and Adam Coates. 2018. Cold fusion: Training seq2seq models together with language models. *ArXiv*, abs/1708.06426.

Ashish Vaswani, Noam M. Shazeer, Niki Parmar, Jakob Uszkoreit, Llion Jones, Aidan N. Gomez, Lukasz Kaiser, and Illia Polosukhin. 2017. Attention is all you need. In *NIPS*.

Shinji Watanabe, Takaaki Hori, Shigeki Karita, Tomoki Hayashi, Jiro Nishitoba, Yuya Unno, Nelson Yalta, Jahn Heymann, Matthew Wiesner, Nanxin Chen, Adithya Renduchintala, and Tsubasa Ochiai. 2018. Espnet: End-to-end speech processing toolkit. *ArXiv*, abs/1804.00015.

Ding Zhao, Tara N. Sainath, David Rybach, Pat Rondon, Deepti Bhatia, Bo Li, and Ruoming Pang. 2019. Shallow-fusion end-to-end contextual biasing. In *INTERSPEECH*.

Semantic Content Prediction for Generating Interviewing Dialogues to Elicit Users' Food Preferences

Jie Zeng
Graduate School of Science
and Technology, Seikei University
dd196201@cc.seikei.ac.jp

Tatsuya Sakato and **Yukiko I. Nakano**
Department of Computer and
Information Science, Seikei University
{sakato, y.nakano}
@st.seikei.ac.jp

Abstract

Dialogue systems that aim to acquire user models through interactions with users need to have interviewing functionality. In this study, we propose a method to generate interview dialogues to build a dialogue system that acquires user preferences for food. First, we collected 118 text-based dialogues between the interviewer and customer and annotated the communicative function and semantic content of the utterances. Next, using the corpus as training data, we created a classification model for the communicative function of the interviewer's next utterance and a generative model that predicts the semantic content of the utterance based on the dialogue history. By representing semantic content as a sequence of tokens, we evaluated the semantic content prediction model using BLEU. The results demonstrated that the semantic content produced by the proposed method was closer to the ground truth than the semantic content transformed from the output text generated by the retrieval model and GPT-2. Further, we present some examples of dialogue generation by applying model outputs to template-based sentence generation.

1 Introduction

Traditionally, dialogue systems have been characterized in terms of whether they are task- or non-task-oriented. In task-oriented dialogue systems, such as an airline ticket reservation system (Hemphill et al., 1990), eliciting specific information from the user, such as the date, time, and destination of the flight, is an important functionality for completing the task. However, in non-task-oriented dialogue systems, the system does not have a clear goal of eliciting information from the user, and the content of the dialogue is free.

In this study, as another type of dialogue system, we focus on interviewing systems, in which the goal is to acquire a user model through a flexible flow of dialogue. Specifically, we propose a method for interviewing a user's preference for food. To generate such dialogues, the system must be able to generate appropriate questions to elicit the user's preferences for food while touching on various topics in the food domain, such as how to eat, how to cook, etc., without limiting the content of the dialogue as a task-oriented dialogue does.

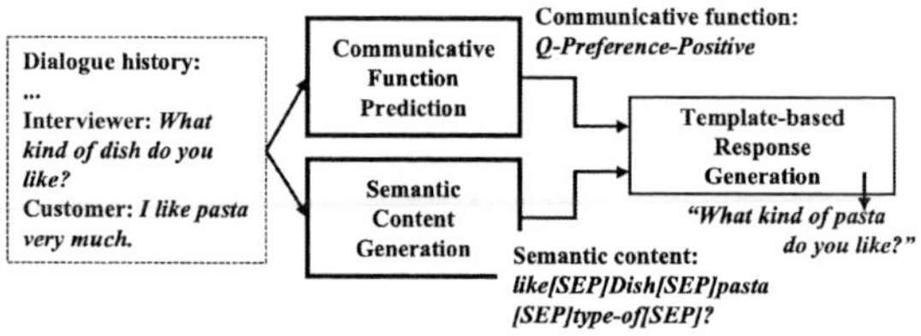

Figure 1: Overview of the proposed method: taking dialogue history as input, a model predicts the interviewer's intent (communicative function), another model decides the content of the utterance (semantic content), and the outputs of these models are combined to generate a response. (For details, refer to Section 4)

One possible approach for achieving the requirements discussed above is end-to-end neural network, where dialogue generation is the task of predicting the next utterance using dialogue history as input (Vinyals and Le, 2015; Serban et al., 2016). This method is widely used to generate open-domain dialogues, such as chitchats. However, it requires a large amount of dialogue data to learn the model. Otherwise, less informative and contextually inappropriate utterances are frequently generated. To overcome this drawback, we propose a method that first determines the intention and semantic content of the interviewer's next utterance and then combines these to generate questions from the interviewer.

Figure 1 shows the proposed approach. First, we trained two models. The first is a classification model that takes the dialogue history as input and determines the interviewer's intention for the next utterance. The second is a generator model, which

Proceedings of the 2nd Workshop on When Creative AI Meets Conversational AI (CAI2), COLING 2022, pages 48–58
October 12–17, 2022.

also takes the dialogue history as input and outputs the semantic content of the utterance, including the target (e.g., dish or ingredient) mentioned in the utterance and its related information (e.g., taste or how to eat). Next, a template for sentence generation is selected based on these two outputs, and they are applied to the selected template to generate sentences. Compared to learning a model that directly generates a surface expression, the models for predicting the intent and semantic content of an utterance can be learned using a smaller amount of data. Additionally, because the content of an utterance is determined based on the context obtained from the dialogue history, appropriate utterances that are related to the preceding utterances can be generated.

The contributions of this study are as follows:

- Collection of 118 text-based dialogues for interviewing food preferences.
- Proposal of an annotation schema for utterance intention and semantic content of utterances, and creation of a dataset with these annotations.
- Creation of a classification model for utterance intention and a generative model of semantic content of utterances.
- Demonstration of the effectiveness of the proposed method using an automated evaluation method.
- Presentation of examples of dialogues generated by the proposed method, and discussion of the quality of the dialogues.

2 Related Work

Task-oriented dialog systems are typically designed to collect information from users. For example, previous studies have proposed an airline ticket reservation system (TIS) (Hemphill et al., 1990), a restaurant reservation system (Henderson et al., 2014), and interview systems to collect information, such as public opinion polls and class evaluation interview systems (Johnston et al., 2013; Stent et al., 2006). In these systems, the purpose of the dialogue is to obtain information to accomplish a predefined task.

Meanwhile, chitchat does not have a clear goal as a task-oriented dialogue does, but this type of dialogue has the potential to elicit a variety of information from the user. For example, the system asks follow-up questions such as "Please tell me more about the *keyword*" by using a keyword from the user's preceding utterance. To improve such interviewing functionality, relevant topics and questions should be selected and the dialogue strategies should be modified. To address these issues, we propose a method to determine the target object and semantic content of the system response based on the dialogue context.

Previous studies on dialogue generation have proposed different techniques to generate task- and non-task-oriented dialogue. Early studies on generating open-domain chitchat proposed DNN-based techniques to generate system responses by exploiting the data-driven approach (Sordoni et al., 2015a; Vinyals and Le, 2015; Serban et al., 2016). Recent studies have proposed incorporating useful information (that is relevant to the domain) and responses into the model, thus improving the quality of generated responses (Li et al., 2018). Some studies have exploited word-based information, such as nouns extracted from the user's preceding utterances and a set of keywords predicted to be used in the response (Serban et al., 2017; Xu et al., 2021). Other studies have used knowledge ontologies, including commonsense (Wu et al., 2020; Zhang et al., 2020; Moon et al., 2019; Galetzka et al., 2021). However, these end-to-end methods, in which training models directly generate system responses, require a large amount of training data, and our corpus was not sufficiently large for this approach.

In traditional task-oriented dialogue systems, the information required to achieve the dialogue goals is limited to the task domain. Therefore, the internal state of the system is defined as a slot–value pair, and the system generates responses through the following modules: a) understanding the user's utterance, b) determining the system action (e.g., the intention and the slot–value as the utterance content) based on the internal state, and c) generating a response sentence from the system action. The action of the system is determined by rule-based, statistical-based (Young et al., 2010), deep learning (Chen et al., 2019) and reinforcement learning approaches (Sankar and Ravi, 2019).

In this study, we exploited the approach described above, which represents the interviewer's utterance as structured semantic content composed of the intent of the utterance, the objects mentioned in the utterance, and their attributes and values. We created a machine learning model to predict these types of information and generate responses based on the determined actions.

3 Data Collection and Dataset Making

This study aims to generate interview dialogues that elicit information about users' food preferences. For this purpose, we collected role-play conversations between an interviewer and a customer and constructed a corpus from the collected conversations.

3.1 Interview Dialogue Collection

Subject pairs were created with participants recruited by crowdsourcing. One subject was assigned the role of an interviewer and the other, the role of a customer. They conducted a text-based chat session in Japanese on the web. After typing an utterance and pressing the send button, the message was added to the chat screen. They were also instructed to take turns sending the messages.

The participants playing as interviewers were requested to engage in conversations to elicit food preferences from customers. The participants playing as customers were asked to indicate their food preferences. We allowed the customers to respond to their real preferences or to pretend to be someone else.

After the dialogue, each participant answered a questionnaire. The interviewers were asked to describe the client's food preferences obtained from the conversation, and the dishes they would like to recommend to the customer. The customers were asked to describe the food preferences they expressed in the dialogue. They were also asked to describe the dishes they would like the interviewer to recommend to them.

To create a dialogue model capable of generating responses that considered the interviewer's dialogue strategy and dialogue history, we requested the participants to input at least 20 turns from each party and 40 turns in total. This was a task completion requirement.

3.2 Annotation

Structured semantic labels were assigned to classify the interviewees' utterances and understand their semantic content. Following the idea of structured semantic labels discussed in the Dialogue Act annotation (Bunt et al., 2012), we represented each utterance as a combination of communicative function and semantic content.

More specifically, a dialog consists of messages sent by the user in the chat, and one message may include multiple sentences. We annotated each sentence in interviewer's message. To annotate sentences in the interviewer's message in our corpus collected in Section 3.1, we first defined labels for communicative function and semantic content.

Communicative Function:

We defined 32 labels for the communicative functions based on those for SWBD-DAMSL (Jurafsky, 1997) and Meguro et al. (2014). We used SWBD-DAMSL to label backward utterances, including understanding, answer, and agreement (Appendix A). For self-disclosure (SD) and questions (Q), we used labels defined in the Meguro et al. (2014) as references and added new labels such as preferences, experiences, and habits. For the preference labels, we added the polarity: positive, negative, and neutral.

Semantic Content:

The semantic content expresses the meaning of a sentence, whereas the communicative function specifies the intention of a sentence, as discussed above. In our corpus, many of the interviewer's questions referred to the name of the dish and its ingredients, tastes, recipes, and how to eat. Based on this observation, we defined semantic content as a combination of utterance objects (e.g., dishes and ingredients) and their attributes (e.g., tastes and cooking methods).

Figure 2 shows the structure of the semantic content and list of values for *<verb>*, *<ObjectType>*, and *<ObjectAttribute>*. Two examples of semantic content were assigned to an interviewer sentence.

In Example A *"I ate hot curry"* in Figure 2, the verb is *"eat"* and its object is *"hot curry"*. The object is the first argument (*argument_1*) of the *verb:eat*, and the relationship between this verb and the object is expressed as a verb frame.

verb frame:

<verb>: We defined five verbs that are frequently used in conversations regarding food. They consider direct objects as arguments. We also defined negative forms for them by adding "!". For example, the negative form for "like" is "!like." In addition to these 10 verbs, "think" and "other" were added, and 12 verbs were defined in total.

object-features:

We defined four types of features for an object. These are *ObjectType*, *ObjectName*, *ObjectAttribute*, and *AttributeValue*. These are

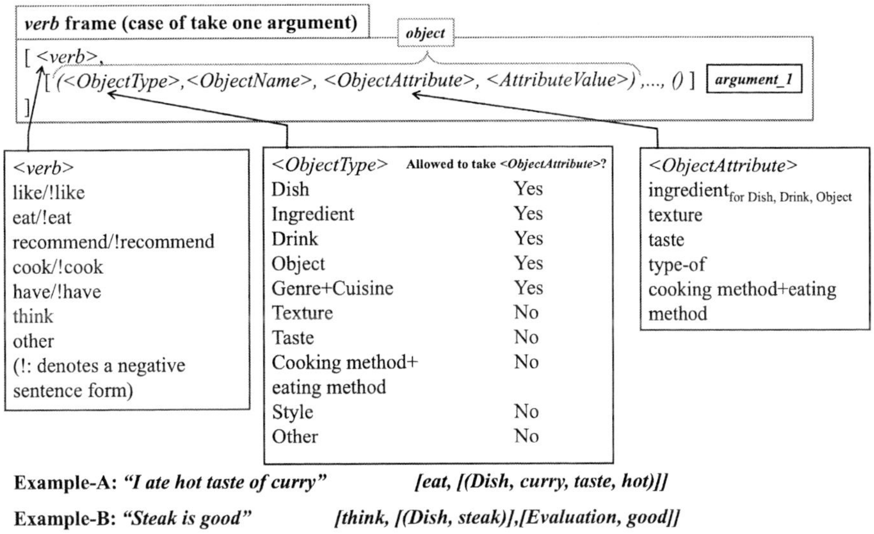

Figure 2: Structure of semantic content and values for <*verb*>, <*ObjectType*>, and <*ObjectAttribute*>. Two examples of interviewer sentence and its semantic content are shown at the bottom of the figure.

called the object features. The *"hot curry"* is an object of the verb *'eat'*. It contains a set of features: *ObjectType='Dish'*, *ObjectName='curry'*,*ObjectAttribute='taste'*, and *AttributeValue='hot'*. We simply expressed this set as *(Dish, curry, taste, hot)*. Details of the object features are presented below.

<ObjectType>: We defined 10 object types: Dish, Ingredient, and Drink. Each name begins with a capital letter. For example, *"Dish"* is assigned as the *ObjectType* value for *curry*, *"Ingredient"* for *carrot*, and *"Genre+Cuisine"* for *Indian food*.

<ObjectName>: This feature indicates the name of the target object in an interviewer's sentence.

<ObjectAttribute>: As shown in Example-A in Figure 2, there are many detailed questions and utterances about the target object, such as the taste of the food, its recipe, and how to eat it. We believe that such information is important for food preferences. To include it in the semantic content, we defined the attributes of objects with a specific *ObjectType*. The values of these attributes are described later in this study.

<AttributeValue>: The value for the *ObjectAttribute* is specified in this section. A set of possible values is not defined, and the value is freely specified, as in *ObjectName*.

For example, the *ObjectType* of *"hot curry"* is a *'Dish'*, and *ObjectType='Dish'* can take an *ObjectAttribute* (see Figure 2, Allowed to take <*ObjectAttribute*>?: Yes). Then, "hot" belongs to *"taste"*, which is defined as an *ObjectAttribute*. As a result, *"hot curry"* is interpreted as an object feature. *ObjectType='Dish'*, *ObjectName='curry'*, *ObjectAttribute='taste'*, *AttributeValue='hot'*.

When the interviewer's utterance is a question, such as a Yes/No question or WH question, the object of the question is indicated as a *'?'*. For example, in the WH question, "What taste of curry do you like?", the *AttributeValue* for *ObjectAttribute='taste'* is the target of this question. In this case, the semantic content is described as *[like, [(Dish, curry, taste, ?)]]* .

For a Yes/No question, where (default) values are already assigned, the features are described as *ObjectName+?* and *AttributeValue+?*. For example, the semantic content for *"Do you like curry hot?"* is described as *[like, [(Dish, curry, taste, hot?)]]*

Some sentences, such as "Steak is good" (Example-B in Figure 2), express an evaluation of the target object. In such a case, "think" is assigned to (<*verb*>), and two arguments are used; the object information is described in *argument_1* and the evaluation in (*argument_2*). In this example, *argument_2* describes a pair of values: "Evaluation" and the (<*EvaluationValue*>) denoting the value of the evaluation. Thus, (*argument_2*) is [Evaluation, good].

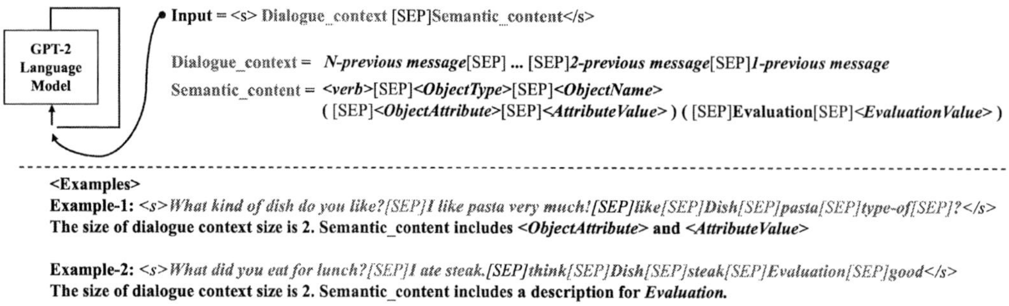

Figure 3: Training a Semantic Content Generation (SCG) model: The description in the parentheses of Semantic_content is used when the target sentence includes the corresponding information.

4 Models

With the goal of building a dialogue system that generates the interviewer's appropriate questions to acquire the customer's food preferences, we present two machine learning models in this section for communicative function prediction and semantic content generation.

4.1 Semantic Content Generation (SCG)

As part of the interviewing system, we created a Semantic Content Generation (SCG) model that generates the semantic content of the interviewer's next sentence. The model takes the history of messages of both the interviewer and customer as input and predicts the semantic content of the last sentence in the next interviewer's message [1]. The representation of semantic content follows the annotation scheme described in Section 3.2.

To train the SCG model, we used a pre-trained Japanese language model [2] of the Transformer-based GPT-2 model (Radford et al., 2019), which is commonly used for conversation generation and fine-tuned it using our own small dataset described in Section 3.1.

Figure 3 illustrates GTP-2 fine tuning to create the SCG model. Each sample of the training data is a pair of dialogue context and semantic content of the interviewer's next sentence. As the dialogue context, messages preceding the prediction target sentence are concatenated. The end of each context message is indicated by [SEP] special token. The maximum number of context messages is five. This sequence is concatenated with the semantic content of the prediction target (the interviewer's sentence) and fed to GPT-2.

The semantic content is represented as a sequence of tokens: verb, object-features, and evaluation description if necessary. Example-1 in Figure 3 shows an example of object-features consisting of *ObjectAttribute* and *AttributeValue*, in which the semantic content of the interviewer's next sentence is *"[like, [(Dish, pasta, type-of, ?)]]"* (original sentence: "What kind of pasta do you like?"). The *verb*, *ObjectType*, *ObjectName*, *ObjectAttribute*, and *AttributeValue* are concatenated into a sequence. Each of these is separated by a [SEP]. Additionally, the <s> and </s> tokens indicate the beginning and end of each sample, respectively. In Example-2, the semantic content contains the evaluation part: *"[think, [(Dish, steak)], [Evaluation, good]]"* (original sentence: "Steak is good."), where the second argument *[Evaluation, good]* is added.

Each input sequence is tokenized by the tokenizer, and GPT-2 optimizes the model weights by minimizing the negative log-likelihood for the next-token prediction.

4.2 Communicative Function Prediction (CFP)

This section proposes a Communicative Function Prediction (CFP) model that predicts the communicative function label to specify the intention of the next interviewer's message, such as self-disclosure and questions.

A fine-tuning approach was employed to train the CFP model. We used the BERT (Devlin et al., 2019) Japanese pre-trained model[3].

[1]When the next interviewer message consists of multiple sentences, the semantic content of the last sentence is used as the prediction target. This is because the main assertion of the message is often made in the last sentence.

[2]japanese-gpt2-small: https://huggingface.co/rinna/japanese-gpt2-small

[3]BERT base Japanese: https://huggingface.co/cl-tohoku/bert-base-japanese-whole-word-masking

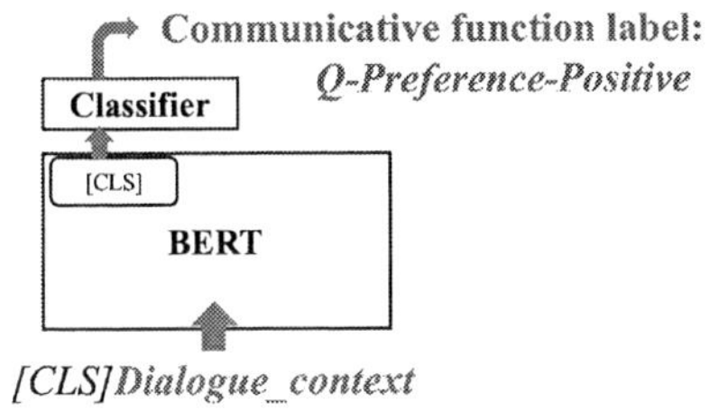

Figure 4: Training a model for communicative function prediction (CFP)

As demonstrated in Figure 4, the input is a dialogue context consisting of multiple previous messages concatenated using [SEP]. This sequence is the same as that used to train the SCG model in Section 4.1. Using this sequence as the input, we trained a model that predicted the communicative function label of the interviewer's next message.

We use the representation of the final layer of the special classification token ([CLS]), which is placed at the beginning of the input, as the input for a downstream classification task. As described in Section 5.1, the communicative function classifier predicts 7 labels, reduced from the 32 labels presented in Section 3.2.

5 Experiments and Evaluation

5.1 Detail of Dataset

Table 1(top) lists the details of the corpus collected in Section 3. Table 1(bottom) shows the number of instances [4] that was used to train the CFP and SCG models. The dataset was divided into train/valid/test sets at a ratio of 7:1:2.

Although we defined 32 communication function labels in the original dataset, many of them were not frequently observed. Thus, we merged the labels whose frequency was lower than 20% of all samples and used the seven labels listed in Table 2 in this experiment.

We calculated the inter-coder reliability using three dialogues annotated by two coders. For the seven labels of communicative function, Cohen's kappa was 0.75, which indicated substantial agreement. For semantic content, which is a combination of verb and object-features, the percentage of agreement was 0.72. Because we achieved a sufficient agreement level, the remaining data were annotated by either coder.

[4]Messages that were not related to the task (e.g., greetings at the beginning of the task, gratitude at the end of the task) were excluded from the dataset.

Table 1: Details of the interview dialogue corpus collected (top) and number of instances used to train the CFP and SCG models (bottom).

# dialogues	118
# messages	4871
- interviewer	2471
- customer	2400
# sentences	8921
- interviewer	4647
- customer	4274

	train/validation/test
# dialogues	84 / 10 / 24
# instances for communicative function	1735 / 209 / 482
# instances for semantic content	1663 / 205 / 458

Table 2: Merged communicative function labels

SD-Fact&Experience	Q-Fact&Experience
Q-Habit	Q-Preference-Positive
Q-Preference-Neutral	Reply
Other	

5.2 Baselines

We compared the proposed models with two baseline models: the retrieval model and text generation model.

Retrieval Model: We simply applied a technique used in information retrieval to a response selection, as proposed in (Ritter et al., 2011; Sordoni et al., 2015b). The customer's message and the interviewer's response to it were paired as an input–response pair. In the response selection process, among all pairs, the one whose input sentence had the highest similarity to the customer's input was selected, and the response part of this pair was used as the system's (interviewer's) response. The sentence vector was a hidden representation of the [CLS] token obtained from BERT, and cosine similarity was used to calculate the sentence similarity.

Text Generation Model: A GPT-2 language model was trained using pairs of dialogue context and the next interviewer's sentence. The difference from the SCG model is that the dialogue context was paired with the text (not the semantic content) of the interviewer's response. Therefore, this model generated an interviewer's response text rather than

Table 3: Average BLEU-4 scores. Numbers in parentheses indicate the length of the dialogue history in the best model using the validation dataset. In the retrieval model, the length of the dialogue history was set to one.

Model	BLEU-4 score (standard deviation)
Retrieval	11.5 (20.6)
Text Generation (N=4)	13.0 (22.3)
SCG (Proposed) (N=3)	**17.3** (24.7)

the semantic content of the sentence.

5.3 Automated Evaluation for SCG

To evaluate the output produced by the models, we conducted an automated evaluation using the BLEU with respect to the semantic content. For this purpose, we treated the semantic content of the target interviewer's sentence as a sequence of words (e.g., *"like[SEP]Dish[SEP]pasta[SEP]type-of[SEP]?"*) and used it as the ground truth.

For the SCG model, the BLEU score was calculated by comparing the generated semantic content with the ground truth. For the retrieval model, the semantic content annotation for the response part was compared to the ground truth. For the text generation model, the semantic content was assigned by annotating the generated message and comparing it with the ground truth to calculate the BLEU score.

As an evaluation of semantic content consisting of a combination of the verb and object-features, we show the average of BLEU scores using 4-grams in the test set in Table 3. The proposed model achieved the highest BLEU score. We changed the dialogue context length from 1 to 5 and found that a model with a dialogue context length of three achieved the best performance in the validation dataset. These results suggest that the proposed SCG model performed the best in reproducing the semantic content of the interviewer's message.

5.4 Performance of CFP

We evaluated the performance of the CFP model by setting the length of the context to three as this setting performed best in the SCG model. The results showed that the model performance for the seven-classes classification was 0.39 in accuracy and 0.30 in weighted average of the F1 score.

5.5 Samples of Generated Response

In this section, we present examples of the responses generated by our interview system. We first describe the template-based response-generation mechanism and then discuss examples of interview generation.

Template-based Response Generation

As shown in Figure 1, the system receives outputs from the SCG and CFP models and generates the interviewer's responses using the template-based generation method.

Suppose that the outputs from the two prediction models are as follows:
communicative function label: *Q-Preference-Positive*
semantic content: *like[SEP]Dish[SEP]pasta[SEP] type-of[SEP]?*

By referring to this information: *communicative function='Q-Preference-Positive'*, *verb='like'*, *ObjectAttribute='type-of'*, and *AttributeValue='?'*, the system selects a template: "*{ObjectName} no Shurui de Nani ga Sukidesuka?*" (in English, "What kind of *{ObjectName}* do you like?"). Then, a response sentence is generated by replacing *{ObjectName}* with the value *'pasta'*.

Discussion on Generated Responses

Table 4 presents the sequence of five context utterances and the interviewer's utterance which follows the context. "Human" is the real interviewer utterance (ground truth). "Retrieval," "Text Generation," and "Proposed" are the outputs by the methods examined in our experiment.

In Dialogue-1 in Table 4, the interviewer utterance generated by the retrieval model asks whether the user eats vegetables. This utterance is not appropriate because in previous-3, the customer had already said that he/she eats vegetables. By contrast, the proposed model generated a question to elicit more information according to the current context of the hot-pot dish by asking the favorite ingredients for the dish.

In Dialogue-2 in Table 4, all three models failed to generate an utterance about the current topic focus (cheese), but the retrieval and text generation models still successfully generated a natural response. However, the utterance generated by the proposed model appears to be abrupt. This is because the selected template was not appropriate or expressive. Providing more templates and improving the template selection mechanism are necessary to generate more expressive responses.

Table 4: Two dialogue examples. Each table contains 5 messages (previous-5 to -1) preceding the prediction target interviewer's sentence, human ground truth responses (Human), and model outputs: Retrieval, Text Generation, and Proposed system. I/C indicates interviewer and customer.

	Dialogue-1
previous-5 (C)	It is strange, isn't it? We hear about rice cake accidents at least two or three times every year, don't we? I would be happy if hormones were a little easier to eat as well, since motsu (pork guts) are delicious and easy to eat.
previous-4 (I)	Do you ever cook hot pot dishes by yourself?
previous-3 (C)	I often make and eat hot pot dishes in winter because it is a good way to get vegetables as well.
previous-2 (I)	Is the hot pot for one person? Do you cook for your family?
previous-1 (C)	I make one for my family.
Human	What do you pay attention to when you cook for your family members?
Retrieval	You mentioned that you can't eat eggplant, but are you a vegetable eater?
Text Generation	Do you like meat?
Proposed	What were your favorite ingredients for the hot pot dishes?

	Dialogue-2
previous-5 (C)	For Korean food, spicy jjigae, chijimi, and bibimbap. I also like to look for good kimchi.
previous-4 (I)	I see. Do you like cheese Dak galbi, which has been getting popular.
previous-3 (C)	I like it because it is a rich taste, as I like cheese. I have even tried to recreate it at home.
previous-2 (I)	That's great! It is a western food, but do you like cheese fondue too?
previous-1 (C)	I love it! I was addicted for a while and bought a cheese fondue pot!
Human	Do you like Hamburg steak with lots of cheese?
Retrieval	Sometimes a sweet treat is okay.
Text Generation	I see. I love it too. I'll try it next time!
Proposed	What is your favorite genre?

6 Conclusion

In this study, we created a dialogue model to interview the food preferences of users. Text-based dialogues between an interviewer and customer were collected, and the communicative function and semantic content of the interviewer's utterances were annotated. Using this dataset, we created models to predict the communicative function of the interviewer's utterances and generate semantic content. The outputs of these two models were then applied to template-based response generation to produce a response. In the model evaluation for generating semantic content, the proposed model outperformed the two baseline models, retrieval and generative, in the automatic evaluation using BLEU-4.

As future work, we will improve the response generation mechanism to generate a variety of expressions because the current template-based response generation may not be sufficient in its expressiveness. For example, one of the ideas would be presenting candidates such as Japanese, Chinese, and Italian when asking about preferences for a genre and asking the user to select one. It would also be useful to predict the user's preference based on the dialog history and user information and generate questions such as "Do you prefer Chinese to Italian? Thus, by using question content (e.g., genre) and related vocabulary and knowledge (Chinese and Italian as examples of genre), the question variation can be increased. Another possibility is to automatically extract or determine the response templates through machine learning, but this is a challenging task.

Further, a user study should be conducted, as it is known that automatic evaluation using BLEU does not always correlate with human evaluation (Liu et al., 2016). In the user study, users interact with the system, and then they evaluate the quality of the responses generated from the system, and judge whether the system effectively elicits information from the user.

Acknowledgements

This work was supported by JST Moonshot R&D Grant Number JPMJMS2011 and JST AIP Trilateral AI Research (PANORAMA project, grant no. JPMJCR20G6) and JSPS KAKENHI (grant numbers JP19H01120 and JP19H04159).

References

Harry Bunt, Jan Alexandersson, Jae-Woong Choe, Alex Chengyu Fang, Koiti Hasida, Volha Petukhova, Andrei Popescu-Belis, and David Traum. 2012. ISO 24617-2: A semantically-based standard for dialogue annotation. In *Proceedings of the Eighth International Conference on Language Resources and Evaluation (LREC'12)*, pages 430–437, Istanbul, Turkey. European Language Resources Association (ELRA).

Wenhu Chen, Jianshu Chen, Pengda Qin, Xifeng Yan, and William Yang Wang. 2019. Semantically conditioned dialog response generation via hierarchical disentangled self-attention. In *Proceedings of the 57th Annual Meeting of the Association for Computational Linguistics*, pages 3696–3709.

Jacob Devlin, Ming-Wei Chang, Kenton Lee, and Kristina Toutanova. 2019. BERT: Pre-training of deep bidirectional transformers for language understanding. In *Proceedings of the 2019 Conference of the North American Chapter of the Association for Computational Linguistics: Human Language Technologies, Volume 1 (Long and Short Papers)*, pages 4171–4186, Minneapolis, Minnesota. Association for Computational Linguistics.

Fabian Galetzka, Jewgeni Rose, David Schlangen, and Jens Lehmann. 2021. Space efficient context encoding for non-task-oriented dialogue generation with graph attention transformer. In *Proceedings of the 59th Annual Meeting of the Association for Computational Linguistics and the 11th International Joint Conference on Natural Language Processing (Volume 1: Long Papers)*, pages 7028–7041.

Charles T Hemphill, John J Godfrey, and George R Doddington. 1990. The atis spoken language systems pilot corpus. In *Speech and Natural Language: Proceedings of a Workshop Held at Hidden Valley, Pennsylvania, June 24-27, 1990.*

Matthew Henderson, Blaise Thomson, and Jason D Williams. 2014. The second dialog state tracking challenge. In *Proceedings of the 15th annual meeting of the special interest group on discourse and dialogue (SIGDIAL)*, pages 263–272.

Michael Johnston, Patrick Ehlen, Frederick G Conrad, Michael F Schober, Christopher Antoun, Stefanie Fail, Andrew Hupp, Lucas Vickers, Huiying Yan, and Chan Zhang. 2013. Spoken dialog systems for automated survey interviewing. In *Proceedings of the SIGDIAL 2013 Conference*, pages 329–333.

Dan Jurafsky. 1997. Switchboard swbd-damsl shallow-discourse-function annotation coders manual. *Institute of Cognitive Science Technical Report.*

Raymond Li, Samira Ebrahimi Kahou, Hannes Schulz, Vincent Michalski, Laurent Charlin, and Chris Pal. 2018. Towards deep conversational recommendations. *Advances in neural information processing systems*, 31.

Chia-Wei Liu, Ryan Lowe, Iulian Serban, Mike Noseworthy, Laurent Charlin, and Joelle Pineau. 2016. How NOT to evaluate your dialogue system: An empirical study of unsupervised evaluation metrics for dialogue response generation. In *Proceedings of the 2016 Conference on Empirical Methods in Natural Language Processing*, pages 2122–2132, Austin, Texas. Association for Computational Linguistics.

Toyomi Meguro, Yasuhiro Minami, Ryuichiro Higashinaka, and Kohji Dohsaka. 2014. Learning to control listening-oriented dialogue using partially observable markov decision processes. *ACM Transactions on Speech and Language Processing (TSLP)*, 10(4):1–20.

Seungwhan Moon, Pararth Shah, Anuj Kumar, and Rajen Subba. 2019. Opendialkg: Explainable conversational reasoning with attention-based walks over knowledge graphs. In *Proceedings of the 57th Annual Meeting of the Association for Computational Linguistics*, pages 845–854.

Alec Radford, Jeffrey Wu, Rewon Child, David Luan, Dario Amodei, Ilya Sutskever, et al. 2019. Language models are unsupervised multitask learners. *OpenAI blog*, 1(8):9.

Alan Ritter, Colin Cherry, and William B. Dolan. 2011. Data-driven response generation in social media. In *Proceedings of the 2011 Conference on Empirical Methods in Natural Language Processing*, pages 583–593, Edinburgh, Scotland, UK. Association for Computational Linguistics.

Chinnadhurai Sankar and Sujith Ravi. 2019. Deep reinforcement learning for modeling chit-chat dialog with discrete attributes. In *Proceedings of the 20th Annual SIGdial Meeting on Discourse and Dialogue*, pages 1–10.

Iulian Serban, Tim Klinger, Gerald Tesauro, Kartik Talamadupula, Bowen Zhou, Yoshua Bengio, and Aaron Courville. 2017. Multiresolution recurrent neural networks: An application to dialogue response generation. In *Proceedings of the AAAI Conference on Artificial Intelligence*, volume 31.

Iulian Serban, Alessandro Sordoni, Yoshua Bengio, Aaron Courville, and Joelle Pineau. 2016. Building end-to-end dialogue systems using generative hierarchical neural network models. In *Proceedings of the AAAI Conference on Artificial Intelligence*, volume 30.

Alessandro Sordoni, Michel Galley, Michael Auli, Chris Brockett, Yangfeng Ji, Margaret Mitchell, Jian-Yun Nie, Jianfeng Gao, and Bill Dolan. 2015a. A neural network approach to context-sensitive generation of conversational responses. In *HLT-NAACL.*

Alessandro Sordoni, Michel Galley, Michael Auli, Chris Brockett, Yangfeng Ji, Margaret Mitchell, Jian-Yun Nie, Jianfeng Gao, and Bill Dolan. 2015b. A neural network approach to context-sensitive generation of conversational responses. In *Proceedings of the 2015 Conference of the North American Chapter of the Association for Computational Linguistics: Human Language Technologies*, pages 196–205, Denver, Colorado. Association for Computational Linguistics.

Amanda Stent, Svetlana Stenchikova, and Matthew Marge. 2006. Dialog systems for surveys: The rate-a-course system. In *2006 IEEE Spoken Language Technology Workshop*, pages 210–213. IEEE.

Oriol Vinyals and Quoc Le. 2015. A neural conversational model. *arXiv preprint arXiv:1506.05869*.

Sixing Wu, Ying Li, Dawei Zhang, Yang Zhou, and Zhonghai Wu. 2020. Diverse and informative dialogue generation with context-specific commonsense knowledge awareness. In *Proceedings of the 58th annual meeting of the association for computational linguistics*, pages 5811–5820.

Heng-Da Xu, Xian-Ling Mao, Zewen Chi, Fanshu Sun, Jingjing Zhu, and Heyan Huang. 2021. Generating informative dialogue responses with keywords-guided networks. In *CCF International Conference on Natural Language Processing and Chinese Computing*, pages 179–192. Springer.

Steve Young, Milica Gašić, Simon Keizer, François Mairesse, Jost Schatzmann, Blaise Thomson, and Kai Yu. 2010. The hidden information state model: A practical framework for pomdp-based spoken dialogue management. *Computer Speech & Language*, 24(2):150–174.

Houyu Zhang, Zhenghao Liu, Chenyan Xiong, and Zhiyuan Liu. 2020. Grounded conversation generation as guided traverses in commonsense knowledge graphs. In *Proceedings of the 58th Annual Meeting of the Association for Computational Linguistics*, pages 2031–2043.

A Communicative Function Set

Communicative function set

SELF-DISCLOSURE(SD-)	Provide own information and opinions about food.
SD-Fact&Experience	e.g., I ate pasta yesterday.
SD-Preference-Positive	e.g., I like oranges.
SD-Preference-Negative	e.g., I don't like fish.
SD-Preference-Neutral	e.g., Coriander is iffy.
SD-Habit	e.g., I often drink coffee.
SD-Desire	e.g., I want to eat pizza.
SD-Plan	e.g., I will have sushi tonight.
SD-Other	
QUESTION (Q-)	Ask questions about their food information and opinions.
Q-Fact&Experience	e.g., What did you eat for breakfast?
Q-Preference-Positive	e.g., What is your favorite dish?
Q-Preference-Negative	e.g., What food do you dislike?
Q-Preference-Neutral	e.g., Can you eat apples?
Q-Habit	e.g., Do you eat eggs often?
Q-Desire	e.g., What do you want to eat for dinner?
Q-Plan	e.g., What are you planning to eat for dinner?
Q-Other	
Proposal	Recommendations. e.g., Chocolate is recommended.
Acknowledge	Encourage the conversational partner to speak. e.g., Huh. Yes.
Appreciation	Express understanding. e.g., Okay. I understand.
Repeat	Repeat the partner's utterance.
Summarize&Reformulate	Paraphrasing, evaluating, and summarizing the partner utterance.
Exclamation	Express emotion utterance. e.g., Oh.
Accept&Agree&Sympathy	Expressing affirmation or agreement.
Partial Accept	Partially expressing affirmation or agreement.
Maybe	Ambiguous utterance. e.g., Maybe so.
Partial Reject	Partially express denial or disagreement.
Reject&Non-Sympathy	Express denial or disagreement.
Greeting	Greeting. e.g., Hello.
Thanks	Express thanks. e.g., Thank you.
Apology	Express apologies. e.g., Excuse me.
Filler	Utterance that fills in the pauses when stuck. e.g., Umm. Well.
Other	Other utterances.

We defined the labels with reference SWBD-DAMSL (Jurafsky, 1997) and Meguro et al. (2014)'s dialogue acts.

Creative Painting with Latent Diffusion Models

Xianchao Wu
NVIDIA
xianchaow@nvidia.com, wuxianchao@gmail.com

Abstract

Artistic painting has achieved significant progress during recent years. Using a variational autoencoder to connect the original images with compressed latent spaces and a cross attention enhanced U-Net as the backbone of diffusion, latent diffusion models (LDMs) have achieved stable and high fertility image generation. In this paper, we focus on enhancing the creative painting ability of current LDMs in two directions, textual condition extension and model retraining with Wikiart dataset. Through textual condition extension, users' input prompts are expanded with rich contextual knowledge for deeper understanding and explaining the prompts. Wikiart dataset contains 80K famous artworks drawn during recent 400 years by more than 1,000 famous artists in rich styles and genres. Through the retraining, we are able to ask these artists to draw artistic and creative paintings on modern topics. Direct comparisons with the original model show that the creativity and artistry are enriched.

1 Introduction

Artistic painting has achieved significant progress during recent years thanks to the appearing of hundreds of GAN variants (Jabbar et al., 2020; Wang et al., 2021). However, adversarial training has been reported to be notoriously unstable and can lead to mode collapse. To escape from adversarial training and inspired by non-equilibrium thermodynamics, diffusion probabilistic models (Sohl-Dickstein et al., 2015), such as noise-conditional score network (NCSN) (Song and Ermon, 2019), denoising diffusion probabilistic models (DDPM) (Ho et al., 2020), stable diffusion models in latent spaces (Rombach et al., 2021) have achieved GAN-level sample quality without adversarial training. These diffusion models are appealing with rather flexible model architectures, exact log-likelihood computation, and inverse problem solving without re-training models.

There are two Markov chain style processes in a typical diffusion model. The first process is a *forward diffusion process* which appends multiple-scale random noise to a given data sample "step by step" or "in jump" until the disturbed sample slip into a predefined isotropic Gaussian distribution. This process does not include trainable parameters. The second process is a *reverse diffusion process* which generates a target distribution data sample from pure noise guided by some (user-input) pre-given conditions. A parameterized deep learning model is required in this reverse process.

Intuitively speaking, the forward diffusion process can be recognized as "directional blasting of a building" $\mathbf{x}_0$ to "ruins with dusts" $\mathbf{x}_T$. The learning algorithm is a *reverse engineering* which learns how to (re-)construct a building (expressed by $p_\theta(\mathbf{x}_{t-1}|\mathbf{x}_t)$ with a parameter set θ and $t \in \{1, ..., T\}$) from each step of *inverse* directional blasting (expressed by $q(\mathbf{x}_{t-1}|\mathbf{x}_t, \mathbf{x}_0)$) of each given building sample $\mathbf{x}_0$. In one step of this reverse engineering, $\mathbf{x}_{t-1}$ represents "one complete wall" in a building and $\mathbf{x}_t$ represents "concrete and sands" that can be used to construct the complete wall $\mathbf{x}_{t-1}$ in a reconstruction process or can be obtained from the complete wall $\mathbf{x}_{t-1}$ in a forward "blasting" process. The reconstruction process is learned from the blasting process with targets such as noise prediction in DDPM (Ho et al., 2020) or score prediction using score matching strategy in NCSN (Song and Ermon, 2019).

We follow a recent impressive work of high-resolution image synthesis with LDMs by given textual or visual conditions[1] (Rombach et al., 2021). There are several proposals in this LDM. The first proposal is applying the encoder part of a pre-trained variational autoencoder to project images into low-dimension latent spaces and then perform

[1] https://github.com/CompVis/stable-diffusion

Proceedings of the 2nd Workshop on When Creative AI Meets Conversational AI (CAI2), COLING 2022, pages 59–80
October 12–17, 2022.

diffusion/construction processes. Training diffusion models on such a low-dimension representation space allows us to reach a near-optimal point between computation complexity reduction and detail preservation to boost virtual fidelity of constructed images. The second is a cross-attention-enhanced (Vaswani et al., 2017) U-Net framework (Ronneberger et al., 2015) in the diffusion model where general conditioning inputs such as text or bounding boxes are taken as *memory* (i.e., keys and values in the cross-attention layers) for the query (latent representations of images to be generated) to retrieve information on. Finally, the decoder module in the variational autoencoder is applied to recover the target image into high-resolution.

We aim at improving the *creativity* of image synthesis, or painting, using conditional LDMs. It is relatively difficult to precisely define the concept of creativity since it is subjective and influenced by culture, history, and region. The color, style, objects included in painting reflect rich emotions of numerous topics. For example, when we are given a textual condition, "a painting of a virus monster playing guitar", we can recognize noun entities such as "virus monster" and "guitar" and a verbal action "playing". What are the emotions involved in this textual hint? Happy, surprise and funny should be the major emotions. The painting requires less imagination since we should better include the entries with a determined action.

However, there are challenges for the models to draw painting for rather high-level topics such as "urbanization of China" or "Asian morning". These textual hints should be enriched and extended with concrete objects and actions to tell a story in a painting or in a series of paintings. Extensions to "urbanization of China" include "originally a collection of fishing villages, Shenzhen rapidly grew to be one of the largest cities in China", "a train runs on the snow-capped mountains of the Qinghai-Tibet Plateau", and "left-behind children running in wheat-field". Given an initial textual hint, we leverage Wikipedia and large-scale pretrained language models to execute this extension.

In addition, we retrain existing checkpoints by the WikiArt paintings dataset[2] which has a collection of 81,444 fine-art paintings from 1,119 artists, ranging from fifteenth century to modern times. This dataset contains 27 different styles (e.g., *Minimalism*, *Symbolism*, *Realism*) and 45 different genres. As far as our knowledge, it is currently the largest digital art datasets publicly available for research usage. This dataset was used to train an ArtGAN (Tan et al., 2017) where conditions such as categorical label information was used for artwork synthesis. In this paper, we embed the textual information of artists, year, styles, and genres as additional conditions to the LDM. Through this way, we can explicitly invite Vincent van Gogh or Rembrant to help us "draw" artworks of modern topics such as "urbanization of China".

This paper is organized as follows. In Section 2, we briefly review the background knowledge required for understanding the stable diffusion models (Rombach et al., 2021). In particular, we describe the two processes defined in DDPM (Ho et al., 2020), the variational autoencoder framework and loss functions used in it (Esser et al., 2020), cross attention enhanced U-Net which acts as the backbone of the diffusion model, and pseudo numerical methods integrated with DDIMs for fast sampling. In Section 3, we describe our proposal of extending users' prompts by pretrained language models and existing knowledge resources. In Section 4, we show detailed information of the Wikiart dataset and our pipeline of retraining. We describe the experiments in Section 5 and finally conclude in Section 6.

2 Background

Diffusion models have been successfully used in image generation (Rombach et al., 2021), text-to-speech synthesis (Popov et al., 2021; Jeong et al., 2021), sing synthesis and conversion (Liu et al., 2021; Xue et al., 2022), music generation (Mittal et al., 2021) and healthcare Medical Anomaly Detection (Wolleb et al., 2022). Surveys can be find in (Croitoru et al., 2022; Cao et al., 2022; Yang et al., 2022).

We limit our discussion to text-to-image generation by leveraging the LDMs (Rombach et al., 2021) and existing checkpoints[3]. We briefly review the core processes and target objectives of DDPMs (Ho et al., 2020) that are used in LDMs. In addition, variational autoencoders enhanced with KL-divergence, cross-attention embedded U-Net (Ronneberger et al., 2015; Vaswani et al., 2017), CLIP pretrained language models (Radford et al.,

[2] `https://www.wikiart.org/` and can be downloaded from `https://archive.org/download/wikiart-dataset/wikiart.tar.gz`

[3] `https://huggingface.co/CompVis/stable-diffusion-v-1-4-original`

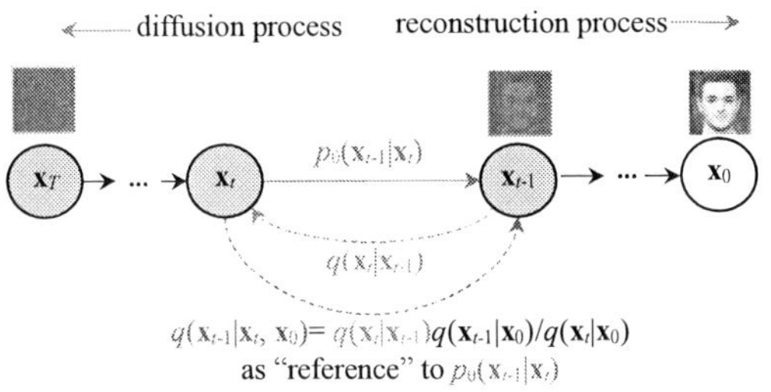

Figure 1: The Markov chain of forward diffusion (backward reconstruction) process of generating a sample by step-by-step adding (removing) noise. Image adapted from (Ho et al., 2020).

2021) and sampling algorithms such as that used in denoising diffusion implicit models (DDIMs) (Song et al., 2020) and pseudo numerical methods (Liu et al., 2022) will be briefly reviewed.

2.1 DDPM

Given a data point $\mathbf{x}_0$ sampled from a real data distribution $q(\mathbf{x})$ ($\mathbf{x}_0 \sim q(\mathbf{x})$), Ho et al. (2020) define a *forward diffusion process* in which small amount of Gaussian noise is added to sample $\mathbf{x}_0$ in T steps to obtain a sequence of noisy samples $\mathbf{x}_0, ..., \mathbf{x}_T$. A predefined (hyper-parameter) variance schedule $\{\beta_t \in (0,1)\}_{t=1}^T$ controls the step sizes:

$$q(\mathbf{x}_t|\mathbf{x}_{t-1}) = \mathcal{N}(\mathbf{x}_t; \sqrt{1-\beta_t}\mathbf{x}_{t-1}, \beta_t\mathbf{I}); \quad (1)$$

$$q(\mathbf{x}_{1:T}|\mathbf{x}_0) := \prod_{t=1}^{T} q(\mathbf{x}_t|\mathbf{x}_{t-1}). \quad (2)$$

When $T \to \infty$, $\mathbf{x}_T$ is equivalent to following an isotropic Gaussian distribution. Note that, there are no trainable parameters used in this forward diffusion process.

Let $\alpha_t = 1 - \beta_t$ and $\bar{\alpha}_t = \prod_{i=1}^t \alpha_i$, we can express an arbitrary step t's diffused sample $\mathbf{x}_t$ by the initial data sample $\mathbf{x}_0$:

$$\mathbf{x}_t = \sqrt{\bar{\alpha}_t}\mathbf{x}_0 + \sqrt{1-\bar{\alpha}_t}\boldsymbol{\epsilon}_t. \quad (3)$$

Here, noise $\boldsymbol{\epsilon}_t \sim \mathcal{N}(0, \mathbf{I})$ shares the same shape with $\mathbf{x}_0$ and $\mathbf{x}_t$.

In order to reconstruct from a Gaussian noise input $\mathbf{x}_T \sim \mathcal{N}(0, \mathbf{I})$, we need to learn a model p_θ to approximate the conditional probabilities to run the *reverse diffusion process*:

$$p_\theta(\mathbf{x}_{t-1}|\mathbf{x}_t) = \mathcal{N}(\mathbf{x}_{t-1}; \boldsymbol{\mu}_\theta(\mathbf{x}_t, t), \boldsymbol{\Sigma}_\theta(\mathbf{x}_t, t)); \quad (4)$$

$$p_\theta(\mathbf{x}_{0:T}) := p(\mathbf{x}_T)\prod_{t=1}^{T} p_\theta(\mathbf{x}_{t-1}|\mathbf{x}_t). \quad (5)$$

Note that the reverse conditional probability is tractable by first applying Bayes' rule to three Gaussian distributions and then completing the "quadratic component" in the $\exp(\cdot)$ function:

$$\begin{aligned} q(\mathbf{x}_{t-1}|\mathbf{x}_t, \mathbf{x}_0) &= \mathcal{N}(\mathbf{x}_{t-1}; \tilde{\boldsymbol{\mu}}_t(\mathbf{x}_t, \mathbf{x}_0), \tilde{\beta}_t\mathbf{I}) \quad (6)\\ &= q(\mathbf{x}_t|\mathbf{x}_{t-1}, \mathbf{x}_0)\frac{q(\mathbf{x}_{t-1}|\mathbf{x}_0)}{q(\mathbf{x}_t|\mathbf{x}_0)} \quad (7)\\ &\propto \exp(-\frac{1}{2\tilde{\beta}_t}(\mathbf{x}_{t-1} - \tilde{\boldsymbol{\mu}}_t)^2). \quad (8) \end{aligned}$$

Here, variance $\tilde{\beta}_t$ is a scalar and mean $\tilde{\boldsymbol{\mu}}_t$ depends on $\mathbf{x}_t$ and noise $\boldsymbol{\epsilon}_t$:

$$\tilde{\beta}_t = \frac{1-\bar{\alpha}_{t-1}}{1-\bar{\alpha}_t}\beta_t; \quad (9)$$

$$\tilde{\boldsymbol{\mu}}_t = \frac{1}{\sqrt{\alpha_t}}(\mathbf{x}_t - \frac{1-\alpha_t}{\sqrt{1-\bar{\alpha}_t}}\boldsymbol{\epsilon}_t). \quad (10)$$

Intuitively, $q(\mathbf{x}_{t-1}|\mathbf{x}_t, \mathbf{x}_0)$ acts as a *reference* to learn $p_\theta(\mathbf{x}_{t-1}|\mathbf{x}_t)$. We can use the variational lower bound (VLB) to optimize the negative log-likelihood:

$$\begin{aligned} -\log p_\theta(\mathbf{x}_0) \leq &-\log p_\theta(\mathbf{x}_0) + \\ &D_{\text{KL}}(q(\mathbf{x}_{1:T}|\mathbf{x}_0) \parallel p_\theta(\mathbf{x}_{1:T}|\mathbf{x}_0)). \quad (11) \end{aligned}$$

Using the definitions of $q(\mathbf{x}_{1:T}|\mathbf{x}_0)$ in Equation 2 and $p_\theta(\mathbf{x}_{0:T})$ in Equation 5, a loss item L_t ($1 \leq t \leq T-1$) is expressed by:

$$\begin{aligned} L_t &= D_{\text{KL}}(q(\mathbf{x}_t|\mathbf{x}_{t+1}, \mathbf{x}_0) \parallel p_\theta(\mathbf{x}_t|\mathbf{x}_{t+1})) \quad (12)\\ &= \mathbb{E}_{\mathbf{x}_0, \boldsymbol{\epsilon}_t}\left[\frac{1}{2 \parallel \boldsymbol{\Sigma}_\theta(\mathbf{x}_t, t) \parallel_2^2} \parallel \tilde{\boldsymbol{\mu}}_t - \boldsymbol{\mu}_\theta(\mathbf{x}_t, t) \parallel^2\right]. \end{aligned}$$

We further reparameterize the Gaussian noise term instead to predict $\boldsymbol{\epsilon}_t$ from time step t's input $\mathbf{x}_t$ and use a simplified objective that ignores the weighting term:

$$\begin{aligned} L_t^{\text{simple}} &= \mathbb{E}_{t\sim[1,T], \mathbf{x}_0, \boldsymbol{\epsilon}_t}\left[\parallel \boldsymbol{\epsilon}_t - \boldsymbol{\epsilon}_\theta(\mathbf{x}_t, t) \parallel^2\right] \quad (13)\\ &= \mathbb{E}\left[\parallel \boldsymbol{\epsilon}_t - \boldsymbol{\epsilon}_\theta(\sqrt{\bar{\alpha}_t}\mathbf{x}_0 + \sqrt{1-\bar{\alpha}_t}\boldsymbol{\epsilon}_t, t) \parallel^2\right]. \end{aligned}$$

In (Rombach et al., 2021), LDMs are proposed so that the diffusion processes are performed in compressed latent spaces through a pretrained variational autoencoder $\mathcal{E}(\mathbf{x}_0)$:

$$\begin{aligned} L_t^{\text{LDM}} &= \mathbb{E}_{\mathbf{z}_0=\mathcal{E}(\mathbf{x}_0), \boldsymbol{\epsilon}_t, t}\left[\parallel \boldsymbol{\epsilon}_t - \boldsymbol{\epsilon}_\theta(\mathbf{z}_t, t) \parallel^2\right] \quad (14)\\ &= \mathbb{E}\left[\parallel \boldsymbol{\epsilon}_t - \boldsymbol{\epsilon}_\theta(\sqrt{\bar{\alpha}_t}\mathbf{z}_0 + \sqrt{1-\bar{\alpha}_t}\boldsymbol{\epsilon}_t, t) \parallel^2\right]. \end{aligned}$$

In order to perform condition-based image synthesis, a pre-given textual prompt (or other formats such as layout) y is first encoded by a domain specific encoder $\tau_\theta(y)$ and then sent to the model to predict ϵ_θ:

$$L_t^{\text{LDM}} = \mathbb{E}_{\mathcal{E}(\mathbf{x}_0),\epsilon_t,t}\left[\| \epsilon_t - \epsilon_\theta(\mathbf{z}_t, t, \tau_\theta(y)) \|^2\right]. \tag{15}$$

Here, $\tau_\theta(y)$ acts as memory (key and value) in the cross-attention mechanism (Vaswani et al., 2017) and can be jointly trained together with ϵ_θ's U-Net framework (Ronneberger et al., 2015) from image-conditioning pairs. In the text-to-image generation task of (Rombach et al., 2021), a 12-layer transformer with a hidden dimension of 768 is used[4] (Radford et al., 2021) to encode textual prompts.

2.2 Variational Autoencoder GAN with KL-divergence

The variational autoencoder is pretrained (Esser et al., 2020) beforehand and used directly for encoding the original data sample into latent space and for decoding the reconstructed $\mathbf{z}_0$ back to the original sizes of $\mathbf{x}_0$. In order to combine the effectiveness of the inductive bias of CNNs with the expressivity of transformers, both the encoder ($\mathcal{E}$) and the decoder (or, generator, $\mathcal{G}$) parts of the autoencoder use ResNet blocks and self-attention blocks. Adversarial learning is used to train this vector quantised GAN framework with a combination of several losses:

(1) a *reconstruction* loss:

$$\mathcal{L}_{\text{rec}} = \| \mathbf{x} - \mathcal{G}(\mathbf{q}(\mathcal{E}(\mathbf{x}))) \|^2, \tag{16}$$

where $\mathbf{q}(\cdot)$ is element-wise quantization in (Esser et al., 2020) and a simple 2D 1×1 convolution network in the stable diffusion implementation. We set $\hat{\mathbf{x}} = \mathcal{G}(\mathbf{q}(\mathcal{E}(\mathbf{x}))$ hereafter.

(2) a *perceptual* loss using the learned perceptual image patch similarity (LPIPS) loss (Zhang et al., 2018):

$$\begin{aligned} \text{Scale}(\mathbf{x}) &= (\mathbf{x} - \text{shift})/\text{scale}, \\ g_i(\mathbf{x}) &= \| \text{VGG}_i(\text{Scale}(\mathbf{x})) \|_2, \\ \mathcal{L}_{\text{per}} &= \sum_{i=0}^{4} \left\{\text{lin}_i((g_i(\mathbf{x}) - g_i(\hat{\mathbf{x}}))^2)\right\}. \end{aligned} \tag{17}$$

Here, "shift" and "scale" respectively stands for mean vector and standard deviation vector of each channel of the images in the training data. A pre-trained VGG checkpoint[5] is used here and VGG_i stands for the i-th layer's output tensor with half-size down sampling shapes (e.g., h, w=256, 128, 64, 32, 16 and c=64, 128, 256, 512, 512). A group of "dropout + conv2d 1×1" (linear) modules lin_i are used project the mean square distances of $\mathbf{x}$ and $\hat{\mathbf{x}}$ into channel number of 1 and then average on height and width. The five scale losses are added up together as the final perceptual loss.

(3) a KL loss between the diagonal Gaussian distribution constructed from $\mathbf{q}(\mathcal{E}(\mathbf{x})) = [\boldsymbol{\mu}; \log\boldsymbol{\sigma}^2]$ and $\mathcal{N}(0, \mathbf{I})$:

$$\mathcal{L}_{\text{KL}}(\mathcal{N}(\boldsymbol{\mu}, \boldsymbol{\sigma}^2) \parallel \mathcal{N}(0, \mathbf{I})) = \sum_{c,h,w} (\boldsymbol{\mu}^2 + \boldsymbol{\sigma}^2 - 1 - \log\boldsymbol{\sigma}^2)/2, \tag{18}$$

where c is channel number, h is height and w is width for an image. The output tensor $\mathbf{q}(\mathcal{E}(\mathbf{x}))$ is separated into two parts (e.g., from (6, 64, 64) to two (3, 64, 64) shape tensors) for the mean and the log of the variance of the Gaussian distribution.

(4) GAN losses which includes the following component:

$$\mathcal{L}_g = -\log\mathcal{D}(\hat{\mathbf{x}}), \tag{19}$$

$$\mathcal{L}_d = \text{Hinge}(\mathcal{D}(\mathbf{x}), \mathcal{D}(\hat{\mathbf{x}})) \tag{20}$$

$$= \frac{\text{relu}(1 - \mathcal{D}(\mathbf{x})) + \text{relu}(1 + \mathcal{D}(\hat{\mathbf{x}}))}{2}. \tag{21}$$

Here, $\mathcal{D}$ stands for a patch-based discriminator that aims to differentiate between real and reconstructed images. Adaptive weight is used to combine these losses and more details can be found in (Esser et al., 2020):

$$\mathcal{L} = \mathcal{L}_{\text{rec}} + \lambda_1\mathcal{L}_{\text{per}} + \lambda_2\mathcal{L}_{\text{KL}} + \lambda_3\mathcal{L}_g + \lambda_4\mathcal{L}_d. \tag{22}$$

In the configuration used in this paper, $\lambda_1 = 1.0$, $\lambda_2 = 1e - 06$. Specially,

$$\lambda_3 = \frac{\nabla_{\mathcal{G}_{\text{last}}}[\mathcal{L}_{\text{rec}} + \lambda_1\mathcal{L}_{\text{per}}]}{\nabla_{\mathcal{G}_{\text{last}}}[\mathcal{L}_g] + \delta}. \tag{23}$$

Here, $\nabla_{\mathcal{G}_{\text{last}}}$ stands for the gradient of the combined reconstruction and perceptual losses with respect to the last layer of $\mathcal{G}$, and $\delta = 1e - 4$ is used for numerical stability. The model sets $\lambda_3 = \lambda_4 = 0.0$ at the first M (e.g., 50,000) iterations to focus on training the reconstruction and perceptual abilities of the model. After M iterations, λ_4 is set to be 1.0 for adversarial learning.

[4] https://huggingface.co/openai/clip-vit-large-patch14

[5] https://download.pytorch.org/models/vgg16-397923af.pth

2.3 U-Net with Cross Attention

In (Rombach et al., 2021), a U-Net with a multi-head cross attention mechanism (Vaswani et al., 2017) is used to predict ϵ_θ with a MSE loss for training (Equation 15). In a typical U-Net implementation, there are five blocks, a *time embedding block* that embeds an input time step t, *input/middle/output blocks* that perform convolutional and self-attention based representations of $\mathbf{z}_t$ and their cross attentions with conditional memory $\tau_\theta(y)$, and finally a *out block* that projects the result tensor back to the shape of $\mathbf{z}_t$.

The *input block* performs a down sampling with a stack of "resnet + spatial transformer" modules (e.g., 12 modules from (channel, height, width) shape of from (4, 64, 64) to (1280, 8, 8)). Then, the *middle block* with "resnet + transformer + resnet" modules links the *input* and *output blocks* without changing the shape of the tensor. Next, the *output block* performs a up sampling with the same number of modules of the input block (e.g., 12 modules from shape (1280, 8, 8) to (320, 64, 64)). There are residual-style shortcut links here: each module's output is sent respectively from the *input block* to the *output block* with the same level. The final *out block* uses a 2D convolutional layer to project the hidden channel number (e.g., 320) back to the original channel number (e.g., 4).

2.4 DDIMs and Pseudo Numerical Methods

DDIMs (Song et al., 2020) generalizes DDPMs via a class of non-Markovian diffusion processes that lead to the same training objective and give rise to implicit models that generate high quality samples much faster. In the non-Markovian forward process, a real vector $\sigma \in \mathbb{R}^T_{\geq 0}$ is introduced to index a family of *inference* distributions:

$$q_\sigma(\mathbf{x}_{1:T}|\mathbf{x}_0) := q_\sigma(\mathbf{x}_T|\mathbf{x}_0)\prod_{t=2}^{T} q_\sigma(\mathbf{x}_{t-1}|\mathbf{x}_t, \mathbf{x}_0);$$
$$q_\sigma(\mathbf{x}_T|\mathbf{x}_0) = \mathcal{N}(\sqrt{\bar{\alpha}_T}\mathbf{x}_0, (1-\bar{\alpha}_T)\mathbf{I});$$
$$q_\sigma(\mathbf{x}_{t-1}|\mathbf{x}_t, \mathbf{x}_0) = \mathcal{N}(\tilde{\boldsymbol{\mu}}(\mathbf{x}_0, \mathbf{x}_t, \sigma_t), \sigma_t^2\mathbf{I});$$
$$\tilde{\boldsymbol{\mu}}(\mathbf{x}_0, \mathbf{x}_t, \sigma_t) = \sqrt{\bar{\alpha}_{t-1}}\mathbf{x}_0 + \sqrt{1-\bar{\alpha}_{t-1}-\sigma_t^2}\frac{\mathbf{x}_t - \sqrt{\bar{\alpha}_t}\mathbf{x}_0}{\sqrt{1-\bar{\alpha}_t}}.$$

The mean function $\tilde{\boldsymbol{\mu}}(\mathbf{x}_0, \mathbf{x}_t, \sigma_t)$ is chosen to ensure that $q_\sigma(\mathbf{x}_t|\mathbf{x}_0) = \mathcal{N}(\sqrt{\bar{\alpha}_t}\mathbf{x}_0, (1-\bar{\alpha}_t)\mathbf{I})$ without depending on σ anymore.

In the generative process of DDIM, the *denoised observation* $\mathbf{x}_0$ is predicted from pre-given $\mathbf{x}_t$ (reverse usage of Equation 3):

$$f_\theta(\mathbf{x}_t, t) := (\mathbf{x}_t - \sqrt{1-\bar{\alpha}_t}\epsilon_\theta(\mathbf{x}_t, t))/\sqrt{\bar{\alpha}_t}.$$

Then, a sample $\mathbf{x}_{t-1}$ can be generated from $\mathbf{x}_t$ via:

$$\mathbf{x}_{t-1} = \sqrt{\bar{\alpha}_{t-1}}f_\theta(\mathbf{x}_t, t) + \sqrt{1-\bar{\alpha}_{t-1}-\sigma_t^2}\epsilon_\theta(\mathbf{x}_t, t) + \sigma_t\epsilon_t. \quad (24)$$

When $\sigma_t = 0$ for all t, the coefficient of ϵ_t becomes zero and samples are generated from $\mathbf{x}_T$ to $\mathbf{x}_0$ with a fixed procedure. The DDIM($\cdot$) is thus defined as:

$$\mathbf{x}_{t-1}, f_\theta(\mathbf{x}_t, t) = \text{DDIM}(\mathbf{x}_t, \epsilon_t, t). \quad (25)$$

To accelerate the reconstruction process and keep the sample quality, DDIMs (Equation 25) are included in pseudo numerical methods (Liu et al., 2022) which treat DDPMs as solving differential equations on manifolds. In (Rombach et al., 2021)'s code implementation[6] (Algorithm 1), a linear multi-step algorithm, the Adams-Moulton method[7], is used. This pseudo numerical algorithm includes a gradient part of 2nd order pseudo improved Euler, 2nd/3rd/4th order Adams-Bashforth methods, and a transfer part of DDIM. Here, the discrete indices $t-1, t+1$ stand for next (e.g., from T to $T-1$) and former time steps, respectively.

3 Textual Condition Extension

We perform textual condition extension by leveraging wikipedia as the knowledge base and large-scale pretrained language models as implicit knowledge graphs. The pipeline is depicted in Figure 2. Given a textual prompt, we first match it with the title list in wikipedia. At the same time, the input prompt is sent to (1) a pretrained language model, T5 (Raffel et al., 2019), to continue writing by taking the given prompt as a prefix hint and to (2) a pretrained dialog model, DialoGPT[8] (Zhang et al., 2019) that takes the input prompt as "query" and consequently generate "responses".

Wikipedia's titles and contents are used for matching the input prompt and T5/DialoGPT's outputs. We use BM25 (Robertson, 2009) here to

[6] https://github.com/CompVis/stable-diffusion/blob/main/ldm/models/diffusion/plms.py#L218 L232

[7] https://en.wikipedia.org/wiki/Linear_multistep_method#CITEREFHairerN%C3%B8rsettWanner1993

[8] https://github.com/microsoft/DialoGPT

Algorithm 1: Pseudo linear multi-step (PLMS) algorithm enhanced by DDIM

$\mathbf{x}_T \sim \mathcal{N}(0, \mathbf{I})$;
for $t = T, T-1, ..., 1$ **do**
  $e_t = \epsilon_\theta(\mathbf{x}_t, t)$;
  if $t == T$ **then**
    # pseudo improved Euler-2nd;
    $\mathbf{x}_{t-1}, f_\theta(\mathbf{x}_t, t) = \text{DDIM}(\mathbf{x}_t, e_t, t)$;
    $e_{t-1} = \epsilon_\theta(\mathbf{x}_{t-1}, t-1)$;
    $e'_t = (e_t + e_{t-1})/2$;
  else if $t == T\text{-}1$ **then**
    # PLMS-2nd (Adams-Bashforth) ;
    $e'_t = (3e_t - e_{t+1})/2$;
  else if $t == T\text{-}2$ **then**
    # PLMS-3rd (Adams-Bashforth) ;
    $e'_t = (23e_t - 16e_{t+1} + 5e_{t+2})/12$;
  else
    # PLMS-4th (Adams-Bashforth) ;
    $e'_t = (55e_t - 59e_{t+1} + 37e_{t+2} - 9e_{t+3})/24$;
  $\mathbf{x}_{t-1}, f_\theta(\mathbf{x}_t, t) = \text{DDIM}(\mathbf{x}_t, e'_t, t)$;
return $\mathbf{x}_0$;

simplify the matching process. From the result document(s), we further compute sentence importance to rank their content fertility and the relationship with the initial prompt. We use the (English) text part of LAION-5B[9] and Wikiart to train a TF-IDF model and then use it to score the prompts in the result prompt list. With a higher score, we subjectively believe that the prompt can possibly yield better images. To score the "relationship" with the initial prompt u, we embed a pair of initial and result prompts by T5 and compute their cosine similarity. Thus, the importance of a result prompt v is computed by:

$$w(v) = \text{TFIDF}(v) + \lambda_1 \text{Cos}(\text{T5}(u), \text{T5}(v)). \quad (26)$$

Here, λ_1 stands for a hyper-parameter to balance the scale of two scores.

In addition, we encourage the result prompts to include spatial and temporal information. We leverage a named entity recognizer[10] and regular expressions to recognize place/region names, addresses, time, and date. The number of spatial and temporal entities discounted by a hyper parameter

[9] https://laion.ai/blog/laion-5b/
[10] https://github.com/kamalkraj/BERT-NER

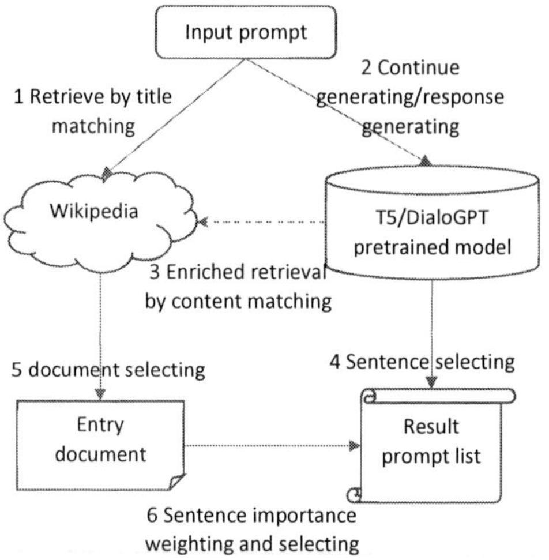

Figure 2: The textual prompt extension pipeline by retrieving wikipedia and continue generating by T5/DialoGPT pretrained language models (Raffel et al., 2019; Zhang et al., 2019).

λ_2 is added with $w(v)$ for the final scoring of a prompt.

4 Retraining with WikiArt

Different artists have quite different numbers of paints in WikiArt dataset. The top-3 artists are Vincent van Gogh, Nicholas Roerich, and Pierre Auguste Renoir with 1,889, 1,860, and 1,400 paintings, respectively. The top-10, top-20, and top-30 artists share 14.18%, 21.80%, and 27.62% of the samples, respectively. Figure 3 shows the distribution of the number of paintings and their authors.

We first retrain the CLIP text encoder with the same tokenizer with the LDM fixed. This stage is expected to map the captions used in Wikiart to stable diffusion's latent space. Then, we fine-tune the text encoder and the LDM jointly. This stage is expected to help the LDM to enrich its knowledge of artworks from different artists, in different styles and genres.

5 Experiments

We use a DGX-A100-80GB server with 8 NVIDIA A100-80GB GPU cards. The original code and settings of the stable diffusion model's checkpoint v1-4 is reused. During inferencing, single GPUs are used with ddim_eta=1.0, ddim_steps=200, height and width are both 512, and scale is set to be 5.0.

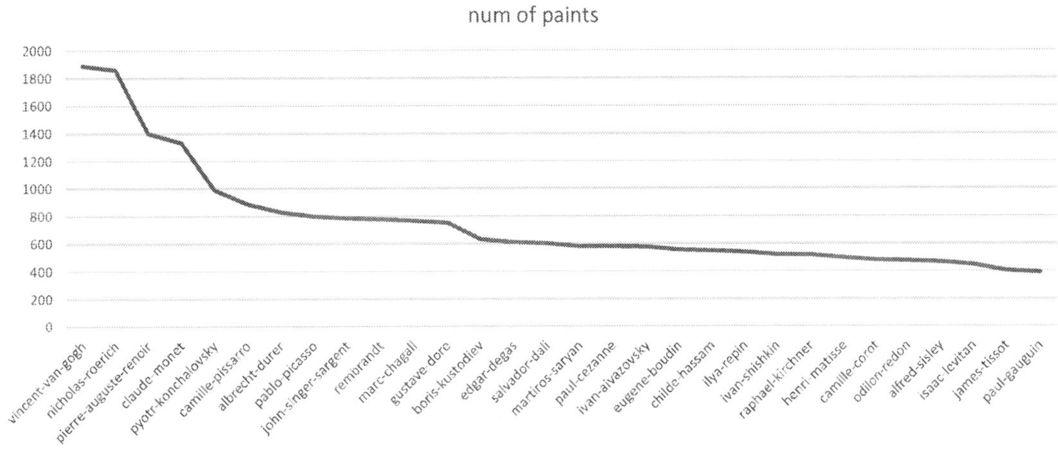

Figure 3: Top-30 artists and their painting numbers in Wikiart.

5.1 Direct Comparison with Original LDMs

Figure 4 directly compares the images generated by the original model and that retrained under Wikiart. We used the same prompts as described in (Rombach et al., 2021). For direct comparison, we also directly copy the first two rows from their original paper. We list four rows picked from the top-30 artists (Figure 3). The painting skills and styles of the artists are reflected. For example, in our first row all "drawn" by Vincent van Gogh, it is relatively easy to distinguish them from other artists: star sky appears often and the Zombie painting is telling a rich story of the author himself.

When the "street sign" is given in the first column, the original paper's two results mainly focused on the photo-style signs themselves. Yet, for the artists, the background's nice street views are also important parts of the final painting, such as the sky, the forest, the building and the people with an orange umbrella. With these hints, we modestly draw a preliminary conclusion that our four paintings (rows 3 to 6) of the first column are more creative and include richer sounding environments and humane information.

Column three, five and six are drawn from prompts which include "fake objects" which do not frequently exist in the real-world. The "half mouse half octopus" is more like photos in the original paper (column 3, first 2 rows), our images are closer to hand-drawn paints. When drawing a "chair that looks like an octopus", all the rows in column six are close to artworks.

The final column can be regarded as an industrial design oriented prompt. With the artists' style and genre included, we can positively imagine that when these paints are printed in real-world T-shirts, people will show their interests of further personalized customization and buy them.

5.2 Textual Condition Extension Results

We use the former example of "urbanization of China" to show the results of textual condition extension. Figure 5 shows four artworks by four famous artists, Vincent van Gogh, Nicholas Roerich, Pierre Auguste Renoir and Claude Monet. Interestingly, the major elements frequently used by artists are also reflected here. For example, the star sky of Vincent van Gogh, the water and boats of Claude Monet. The major elements included in the four paintings are also interesting, combinations of Chinese traditional buildings and skyscrapers, combinations of individual houses and mountains, rather crowded endless buildings and blurry sky, and Chinese traditional building style boats with super high skyscrapers around the rivers.

Figure 6 shows the same four artists' artwork for an extended prompt related to one of the most rapidly developed cities, Shenzhen, during the urbanization of China. With the extended prompts, the model could generate more expressive images. For Vincent van Gogh, a moon in the middle of the sky, with fishing-boats near and high buildings in the far view. The same elements of fish boats and skyscrapers are all included in the other three paintings. Interestingly, for Nicholas Roerich, even the skyscrapers are drawn by following traditional Chinese style.

Figure 7 shows the same four artists' artwork for an extended prompt related to a train running on the snow-capped mountains, during the urbanization of China. With the extended prompts, again, the model could generate more expressive images and keep the characters of each artist. The general styles and viewpoints of the four artists are reflected: now we have the mountain as the "sky" of Vincent van Gogh and the "sky and mountain" in Claude Monet looks like a reversed river.

Figure 8 shows the same four artists' artwork for an extended prompt related to children running in wheat-fields, during the urbanization of China. With the extended prompts, again, the model could generate more expressive images with rich emotional colors such as blue skies, golden wheat fields, and running-enjoy children. The general styles and viewpoints of the four artists are reflected, such as Vincent van Gogh's sky and the skirts of the two girls from Claude Monet.

Full images of the top-30 artists (Figure 4) of the one initial prompt and three extended prompts are shown in Figure 9, 10, 11 and 12 respectively.

5.3 Diversity and Styles

We finally investigate the diversity and style influences. Figures 13, 14, 15 and 16 shows the 27 styles of Vincent van Gogh, each style with 5 samples (per row), for the former prompt "left-behind children running in wheat-field". Most images are with a "van Gogh" style sky. The diversity is ensured by comparing the columns in each row. Since Vincent van Gogh is famous for "Post Impressionism" (Figure 16, row 2), the characteristics of other styles are relatively less recognizable. The balancing of between keeping the typical style of van Gogh and introducing new styles is relatively difficult. Still, from the five images of style "Ukiyo e" (Figure 14, row 2), we can recognize that the children are with Japanese traditional cloths and hair styles (so do the buildings behind).

6 Conclusion

In order to improve the creativity of LDMs, we have proposed two directions of extending the input prompts and of retraining the original model by the Wikiart dataset. We take the 1,000 artists in recent 400 years as the major source of both creativity and artistry. With these proposals, the resulting diffusion models can ask these famous artists to draw novel and expressive paints of modern topics.

We believe this is an interesting topic and has industrial design requirements for real-world applications, such as cloth designing, advertisement posters, and game character designing. Through drawing the real-world's topics with the help of hundreds to thousands famous artists, it is reasonable to learn the creativity and fertility from these artists' eyes.

References

Hanqun Cao, Cheng Tan, Zhangyang Gao, Guangyong Chen, Pheng-Ann Heng, and Stan Z. Li. 2022. A survey on generative diffusion model.

Florinel-Alin Croitoru, Vlad Hondru, Radu Tudor Ionescu, and Mubarak Shah. 2022. Diffusion models in vision: A survey.

Patrick Esser, Robin Rombach, and Björn Ommer. 2020. Taming transformers for high-resolution image synthesis. *CoRR*, abs/2012.09841.

Jonathan Ho, Ajay Jain, and Pieter Abbeel. 2020. Denoising diffusion probabilistic models. *CoRR*, abs/2006.11239.

Abdul Jabbar, Xi Li, and Bourahla Omar. 2020. A survey on generative adversarial networks: Variants, applications, and training. *CoRR*, abs/2006.05132.

Myeonghun Jeong, Hyeongju Kim, Sung Jun Cheon, Byoung Jin Choi, and Nam Soo Kim. 2021. Diff-tts: A denoising diffusion model for text-to-speech.

Luping Liu, Yi Ren, Zhijie Lin, and Zhou Zhao. 2022. Pseudo numerical methods for diffusion models on manifolds.

Songxiang Liu, Yuewen Cao, Dan Su, and Helen Meng. 2021. Diffsvc: A diffusion probabilistic model for singing voice conversion.

Gautam Mittal, Jesse H. Engel, Curtis Hawthorne, and Ian Simon. 2021. Symbolic music generation with diffusion models. *CoRR*, abs/2103.16091.

Vadim Popov, Ivan Vovk, Vladimir Gogoryan, Tasnima Sadekova, and Mikhail A. Kudinov. 2021. Grad-tts: A diffusion probabilistic model for text-to-speech. *CoRR*, abs/2105.06337.

Alec Radford, Jong Wook Kim, Chris Hallacy, Aditya Ramesh, Gabriel Goh, Sandhini Agarwal, Girish Sastry, Amanda Askell, Pamela Mishkin, Jack Clark, Gretchen Krueger, and Ilya Sutskever. 2021. Learning transferable visual models from natural language supervision. *CoRR*, abs/2103.00020.

Colin Raffel, Noam Shazeer, Adam Roberts, Katherine Lee, Sharan Narang, Michael Matena, Yanqi Zhou, Wei Li, and Peter J. Liu. 2019. Exploring the limits of transfer learning with a unified text-to-text transformer. *CoRR*, abs/1910.10683.

S. Robertson. 2009. The Probabilistic Relevance Framework: BM25 and Beyond. *Foundations and Trends® in Information Retrieval*, 3(4):333–389.

Robin Rombach, Andreas Blattmann, Dominik Lorenz, Patrick Esser, and Björn Ommer. 2021. High-resolution image synthesis with latent diffusion models. *CoRR*, abs/2112.10752.

Olaf Ronneberger, Philipp Fischer, and Thomas Brox. 2015. U-net: Convolutional networks for biomedical image segmentation. *CoRR*, abs/1505.04597.

Jascha Sohl-Dickstein, Eric A. Weiss, Niru Maheswaranathan, and Surya Ganguli. 2015. Deep unsupervised learning using nonequilibrium thermodynamics. *CoRR*, abs/1503.03585.

Jiaming Song, Chenlin Meng, and Stefano Ermon. 2020. Denoising diffusion implicit models. *CoRR*, abs/2010.02502.

Yang Song and Stefano Ermon. 2019. Generative modeling by estimating gradients of the data distribution. In *Advances in Neural Information Processing Systems*, volume 32. Curran Associates, Inc.

Wei Ren Tan, Chee Seng Chan, Hernán E. Aguirre, and Kiyoshi Tanaka. 2017. Artgan: Artwork synthesis with conditional categorial gans. *CoRR*, abs/1702.03410.

Ashish Vaswani, Noam Shazeer, Niki Parmar, Jakob Uszkoreit, Llion Jones, Aidan N Gomez, Ł ukasz Kaiser, and Illia Polosukhin. 2017. Attention is all you need. In *Advances in Neural Information Processing Systems*, volume 30. Curran Associates, Inc.

Zhengwei Wang, Qi She, and Tomas Ward. 2021. Generative adversarial networks in computer vision: A survey and taxonomy. *ACM Computing Surveys*, 54:1–38.

Julia Wolleb, Florentin Bieder, Robin Sandkühler, and Philippe C. Cattin. 2022. Diffusion models for medical anomaly detection.

Heyang Xue, Xinsheng Wang, Yongmao Zhang, Lei Xie, Pengcheng Zhu, and Mengxiao Bi. 2022. Learn2sing 2.0: Diffusion and mutual information-based target speaker svs by learning from singing teacher.

Ling Yang, Zhilong Zhang, Shenda Hong, Runsheng Xu, Yue Zhao, Yingxia Shao, Wentao Zhang, Ming-Hsuan Yang, and Bin Cui. 2022. Diffusion models: A comprehensive survey of methods and applications.

Richard Zhang, Phillip Isola, Alexei A. Efros, Eli Shechtman, and Oliver Wang. 2018. The unreasonable effectiveness of deep features as a perceptual metric. *CoRR*, abs/1801.03924.

Yizhe Zhang, Siqi Sun, Michel Galley, Yen-Chun Chen, Chris Brockett, Xiang Gao, Jianfeng Gao, Jingjing Liu, and Bill Dolan. 2019. Dialogpt: Large-scale generative pre-training for conversational response generation. *CoRR*, abs/1911.00536.

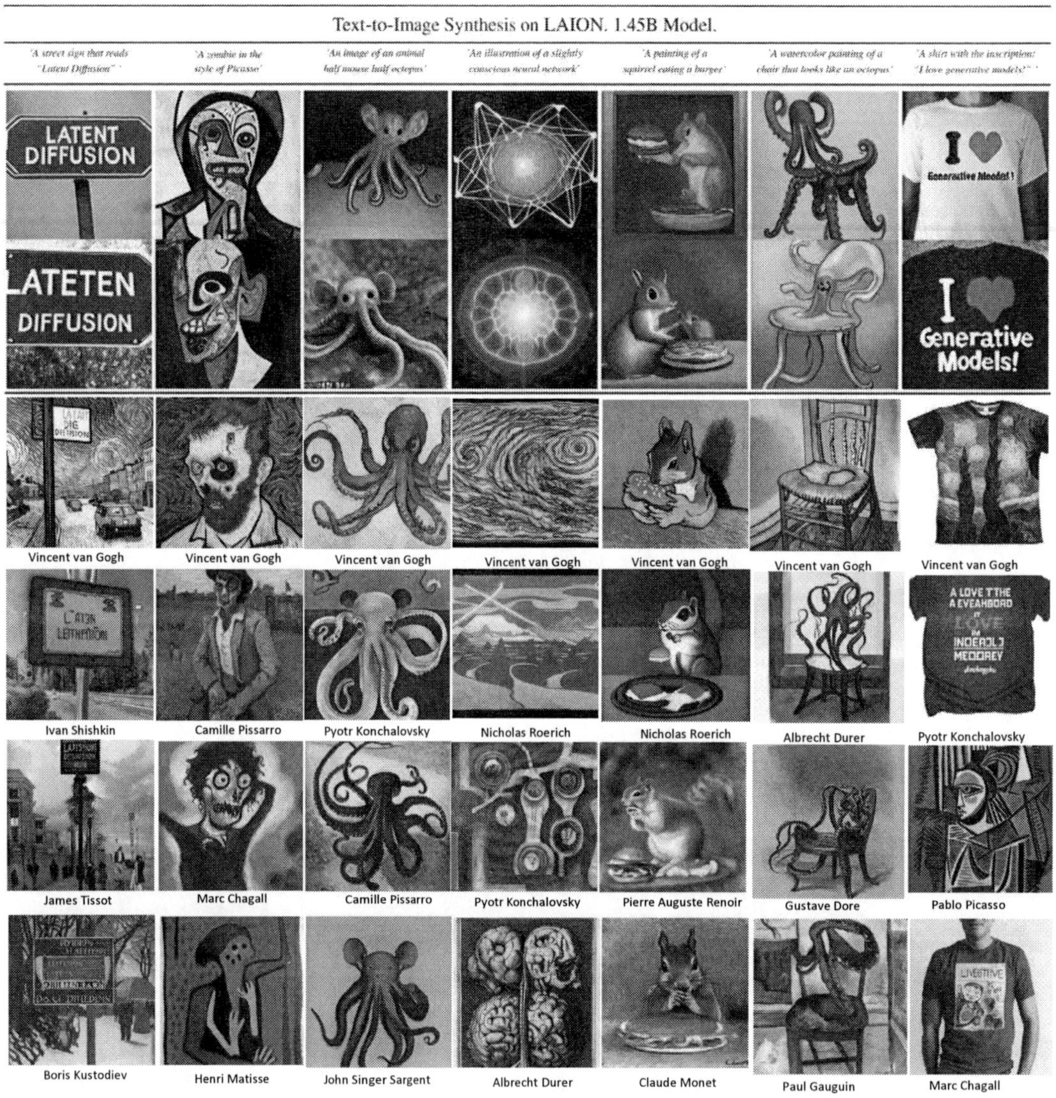

Figure 4: Direct comparison with the same prompts used in (Rombach et al., 2021) yet different artists.

Figure 5: Four artists' artworks for the same prompt of "a painting of urbanization of china".

Figure 6: Four artists' artworks for the same extended prompt of "originally a collection of fishing villages, Shenzhen rapidly grew to be one of the largest cities in China".

Vincent van Gogh

Nicholas Roerich

Pierre Auguste Renoir

Claude Monet

Figure 7: Four artists' artworks for the same extended prompt of "a train runs on the snow-capped mountains of the Qinghai-Tibet Plateau".

Figure 8: Four artists' artworks for the same extended prompt of "left-behind children running in wheat-field".

Figure 9: Top-30 artists' artworks for the same extended prompt of "a painting of urbanization of china".

Figure 10: Top-30 artists' artworks for the same extended prompt of "originally a collection of fishing villages, Shenzhen rapidly grew to be one of the largest cities in China".

Figure 11: Top-30 artists' artworks for the same extended prompt of "a train runs on the snow-capped mountains of the Qinghai-Tibet Plateau".

Figure 12: Top-30 artists' artworks for the same extended prompt of "left-behind children running in wheat-field".

Figure 13: Vincent van Gogh's seven styles (Minimalism, Abstract Expressionism Fauvism, Naive Art Primitivism, Symbolism, Color Field Painting, Pointillism), each style with five samples (per row).

Figure 14: Vincent van Gogh's seven styles (Baroque, Ukiyo e, Early Renaissance, Action painting, Contemporary Realism, Mannerism Late Renaissance, Analytical Cubism), each style with five samples (per row).

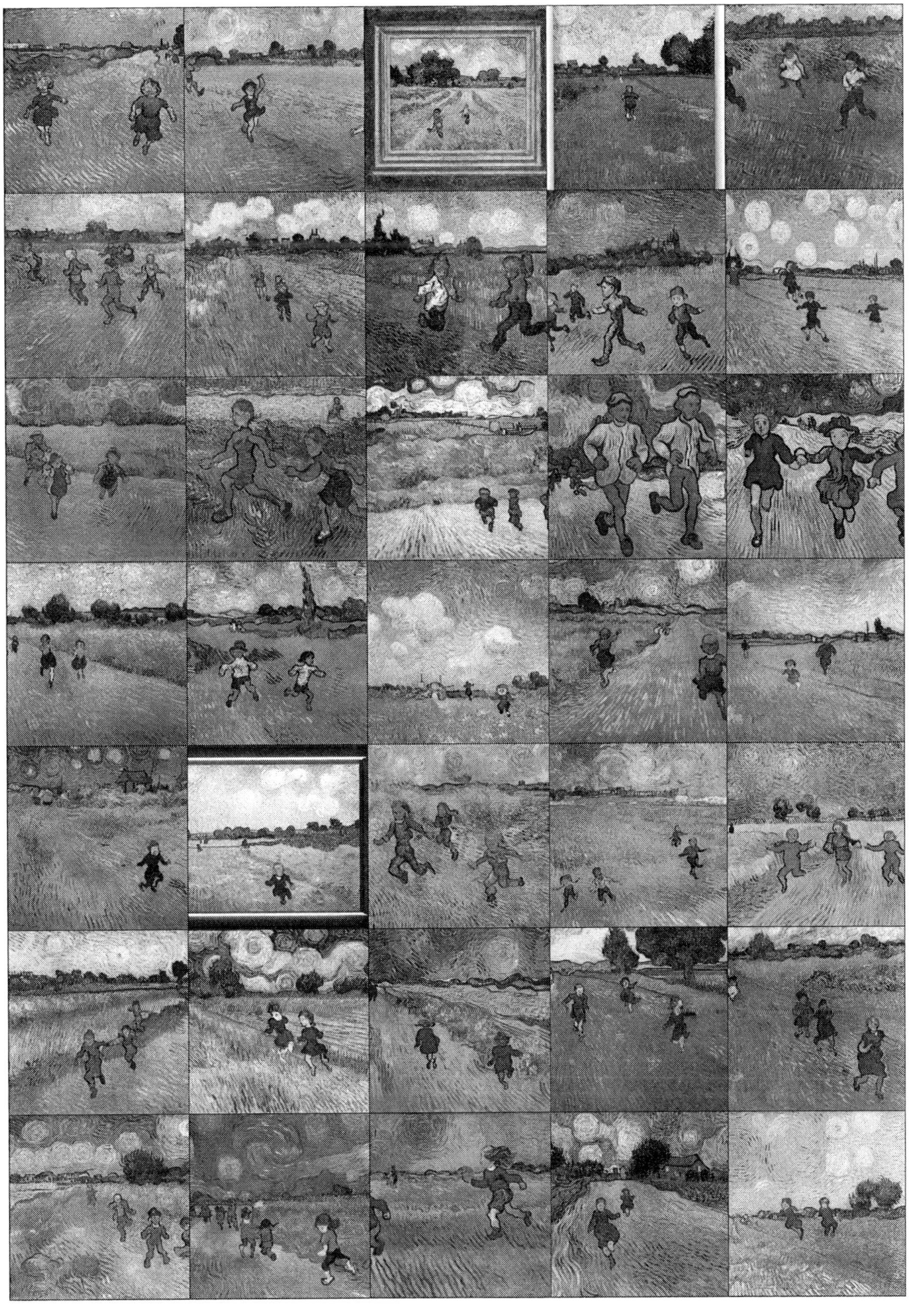

Figure 15: Vincent van Gogh's seven styles (New Realism, Northern Renaissance, Cubism Impressionism, Expressionism, Realism, High Renaissance), each style with five samples (per row).

Figure 16: Vincent van Gogh's six styles (Pop Art, Post Impressionism, Synthetic Cubism Art Nouveau Modern, Rococo, Romanticism,), each style with five samples (per row).

Learning to Evaluate Humor in Memes Based on the Incongruity Theory

Kohtaro Tanaka[1], **Hiroaki Yamane**[2,1], **Yusuke Mori**[1], **Yusuke Mukuta**[1,2], **Tatsuya Harada**[1,2]
[1]The University of Tokyo [2]RIKEN
{k-tanaka, yamane, mori, mukuta, harada}@mi.t.u-tokyo.ac.jp

Abstract

Memes are a widely used means of communication on social media platforms, and are known for their ability to "go viral". In prior works, researchers have aimed to develop an AI system to understand humor in memes. However, existing methods are limited by the reliability and consistency of the annotations in the dataset used to train the underlying models. Moreover, they do not explicitly take advantage of the incongruity between images and their captions, which is known to be an important element of humor in memes. In this study, we first gathered real-valued humor annotations of 7,500 memes through a crowdwork platform. Based on this data, we propose a refinement process to extract memes that are not influenced by interpersonal differences in the perception of humor and a method designed to extract and utilize incongruities between images and captions. The results of an experimental comparison with models using vision and language pretraining models show that our proposed approach outperformed other models in a binary classification task of evaluating whether a given meme was humorous.

Figure 1: An example of a meme from a meme-sharing website "Best of funny memes"[1].

1 Introduction

Humor is an essential element of human communication. Studies have shown that humor helps to build relationships in work environments (Plester, 2009), facilitates smooth discussions on controversial topics (McGhee, 1989), and helps motivate people to recognize and challenge misinformation (Yeo and McKasy, 2021).

Memes are a type of humor that has been prevalent in recent years, especially on social media. These images express multi-modal humor and often comprise a template image with superimposed upper and lower captions. In the example of a meme shown in Figure 1, the upper caption reads "JOIN THE MARINES THEY SAID" and the lower caption reads "YOU'LL BE A HERO THEY SAID". Both upper and lower captions are superimposed onto the template image of a marine in dress uniform holding an umbrella for the former president Barack Obama. The humor of memes can be explained by the incongruity theory (Raskin, 1985; Buijzen and Valkenburg, 2004). It is a well-established humor theory which states that a surprising contradiction or opposition to an expected situation or interpretation is a key element of any humor. For example, the meme shown in Figure 1 has an incongruity between the caption and the template image; the caption explains the commonsense of viewers that a marine would be a hero in the battleground, but the image is showing the contradicting reality of a marine doing a boring job of holding an umbrella for the president. A study on incongruities in memes has shown that a large number of memes have image-caption incongruity (Yus, 2021).

Given the substantial impact of memes on online communication, such as their effectiveness in correcting misinformation (Vraga et al., 2019; Kim et al., 2021a; Garrett and Poulsen, 2019), researchers have aimed to develop AI systems capable of understanding humor in memes. However, the evaluation of memes has proven a difficult task.

[1]https://www.funny-memes.org/2013/05/join-marines-they-said-youll-be-hero.html

Proceedings of the 2nd Workshop on When Creative AI Meets Conversational AI (CAI2), COLING 2022, pages 81–93
October 12–17, 2022.

Humor is subjective, and interpersonal differences may affect the perception of humor for some memes based on viewers' cultural background and personality characteristics (Ruch and Hehl, 2010). Hence, human-annotated datasets of humor in memes tend to exhibit inconsistent annotations. In addition, existing methods use vision-language pretraining models that do not explicitly extract semantic relationships between images and captions. As a result of this structure, utilizing image-caption incongruity is relatively difficult with such models, although incongruity was shown to be a significant element in humor of memes (Yus, 2021).

In the present work, we addressed the inconsistency of annotations by first creating a meme dataset with a humor annotation of memes that is not influenced by interpersonal differences in the perception of humor. These reliable humor annotations were obtained via an annotation method called best-worst scaling (BWS) (Louviere, 1992). Then, the annotations were refined by our proposed process to eliminate inconsistent examples. The consistency of each annotation was measured by quantifying the agreement of annotations between different annotators.

Based on this data, we propose a method that explicitly extracts and utilizes image-caption incongruities. Our proposed method combines a vision-language transformer with a module designed to extract the features of image-caption similarity. We validated the performance of our proposed method by conducting experiments in which we used several models for comparison to classify whether a given meme (template image + caption) was humorous.

The contributions of this study are summarized as follows.

- We created a reliable dataset of memes with annotations that quantified their degree of humor and extracted humor anchors.
- We proposed and implemented a dataset refinement process to separate memes influenced by interpersonal differences in the perception of humor. The consistency of the annotations was thoroughly examined.
- We implemented models to explicitly extract image-caption incongruities and compared their output with the baselines implemented based on pretrained vision-language models. We showed that our proposed method outperformed baselines in evaluating the humor of memes.

2 Related Work

2.1 Computational Humor Models

Due to the importance of humor in human communication, several previous studies have aimed to recognize or generate humor of a single modality. These include research on fixed forms of language-based humor such as "*I like my X like I like my Y, Z*" jokes (Petrović and Matthews, 2013), Knock-Knock Jokes (Rayz, 2004), miscellaneous short-text humor (Annamoradnejad and Zoghi, 2020), humor in dialogues (Ziser et al., 2020; Yoshikawa and Iwakura, 2020), and visual humor (Chandrasekaran et al., 2016).

However, few studies have considered multimodal humor, such as humor in memes. One study focused on the task of meme evaluation is a competition called "Memotion Analysis" (Sharma et al., 2020). This competition included the task of predicting the degree of humor of a given meme. The best-performing model adopted several pretrained feature extractors and ensemble techniques (Guo et al., 2020). However, the feature extractors were all unimodal and trained independently. Therefore, these methods do not explicitly utilize semantic relationships between images and captions.

2.2 Humor Dataset

Several methods have been developed to record human annotations of humorous content, including rating scales and BWS (Louviere, 1992).

A rating scale presents annotators with a scale and choices of integers or characters that represent a place within the scale. For example, the dataset used for the competition "Memotion Analysis" (Sharma et al., 2020) was annotated using a rating scale. Annotators were provided with four choices to choose from: not funny, funny, very funny, and hilarious.

Although this method is widely used in various disciplines, rating scales are said to have limitations, including the following (Schuman and Presser, 1996; Baumgartner and Steenkamp, 2001).

- Annotation inconsistencies between different annotators.
- Annotation inconsistencies by the same annotator.
- Bias in selection within the scale.

BWS was proposed to resolve these limitations and reduce the number of tasks required. BWS usually asks annotators to choose the best- and worst-fitting items from among four-tuples of items for the characteristics of interest. Real-valued annotations (BWS scores) can be acquired using maximum difference scaling (MaxDiff) (Finn and Louviere, 1992), a method to conduct and process BWS. To obtain real-valued scores of N items, $[1.5N, 2.0N]$ four-tuples of items were annotated so that each item was evaluated more than about five times. Then, a BWS score was calculated for an item A by subtracting the number of times A was selected as best-fitting by the number of times it was selected as worst-fitting, and dividing the result by the number of times A was evaluated.

The score obtained using this equation is a real value ranging from -1 (worst) to 1 (best).

This method has been proven to produce more reliable annotations compared to rating scales (Kiritchenko and Mohammad, 2017), and has also been used to evaluate the humor of jokes of the form "*I like my X like I like my Y, Z*" (Yamane et al., 2021).

3 Dataset Construction

To construct our reliable dataset, we first obtained a collection of memes from a meme-sharing website. Then, the memes were annotated by crowdworkers. Finally, the annotations were filtered and refined to eliminate inconsistent annotations. As a result, we compiled 1,450 memes with reliable and consistent annotations.

3.1 Data Collection and Preprocess

To create the dataset, we first scraped 693,465 memes (3,000 template images, 143 - 300 captions per template) from Meme Generator[2]. The scraped memes were selected in order of the number of likes they had received to ensure that the dataset included sufficient high-quality memes.

Before asking crowdworkers to annotate the humor in these memes, we conducted preprocessing to reduce the number of memes containing words that were not in English or that were profane.

First, to minimize the number of captions that were not in English, we checked whether each caption could be encoded only using ASCII characters. This filtering process eliminated captions written in languages that do not use ASCII characters and also removed emojis. However, it was not possible to eliminate captions written in languages that use the same alphabet as English, such as Spanish. Although it would be possible to strictly filter captions by checking whether all the included words were present in an English dictionary, we chose not to adopt this approach as meme captions often contain slang or deliberately misspelled words that do not appear in any English dictionary.

As we asked crowdworkers to annotate the humor in memes, we needed to minimize their exposure to profanity. Therefore, we used an open-source library called "profanity-filter" to detect and filter profanity[3]. Although this library enabled the filtration of major profanities, it was not possible to remove inappropriate words that were misspelled or partially concealed.

Finally, image templates that contained more than 150 captions after the two filtering processes were selected and compiled. The resulting preprocessed data contained 296,850 memes (1,979 image templates with 150 captions per template).

3.2 Human Annotation Task Using BWS

To obtain real-valued reliable humor annotations for these memes, we asked crowdworkers on Amazon Mechanical Turk (AMT)[4] to complete three tasks, including answering whether a meme was in English, choosing up to three words that were essential to understanding the humor in the meme, and choosing the most and least humorous meme from among four memes. In our research, we annotated 7,500 memes (100 template images with 75 captions per template) by creating 11,250 four-tuples (1.5N).

Annotation tasks were published on AMT and included two sections with a total of 27 questions.

Section 1 (questions 1 - 24) first asked annotators about their understanding of the meme provided. This question aimed to filter memes that were not in English and not filtered in the preprocessing phase.

Then, annotators were asked to write up to three words in the caption that were necessary to understand the meme (we refer to this data as a humor anchor). If the meme presented was not in English, they were instructed to write "NIE" (not in English) in the first box and leave the other boxes blank. This question aimed to extract humor anchors for each meme and also to evaluate the quality of the annotation (For example, if an annotator chose words that were obviously not important, such as "the", we

[2]https://memegenerator.net/

[3]https://pypi.org/project/profanity-filter/

[4]https://www.mturk.com/

concluded that annotations provided by that worker might be of low quality).

Finally, in Section 2 (questions 25 - 27), annotators were asked to choose the most and least humorous meme from among the four presented. The examples of questions that were presented to the annotators are listed in the appendix.

To ensure the quality of the annotations, the task required workers to be located in the U.S., to have a Human Intelligence Task (HIT) Approval Rate greater than or equal to 98%, and to have at least 500 HITs previously approved. In addition, workers were warned beforehand that the task may contain adult content, as the "profanity filter" did not suffice to eliminate all memes with explicit words.

3.3 Post-process

The resulting annotations were first processed to calculate and compile their BWS scores to obtain the raw dataset.

To ensure the quality of the annotations, the following additional post-processing was performed to produce the post-processed dataset.

- Only the annotations on which workers spent more than ten seconds per question were used.
- Memes which annotators identified as "Not in English" were not used.
- Only memes annotated by more than three people annotated after the other two post-processes were conducted, were used.

This filtering process has reduced the number of human-annotated memes to 6,900 for the post-processed dataset.

3.4 Refining to Filter-out Interpersonal Differences in Perception of Humor

As previous studies have shown that perceptions of humor may be influenced by individual personality characteristics, we analyzed the correlation between differences in BWS score (d) and human agreement (a) to explore how this influence affected our dataset. To do so, we first derived a total of 39,045 hierarchical pairs from the 7,809 annotated four-tuples which were used to create the post-processed dataset. (For example, when an annotator chose A as most humorous and D as least humorous from among four choices A, B, C, D, we derived five hierarchical pairs $A > B$, $A > C$, $A > D$, $B > D$, and $C > D$.) Then, for the 39,045 pairs that were retrieved, d was defined as follows, given the calculated BWS scores of meme A (S_a) and B (S_b).

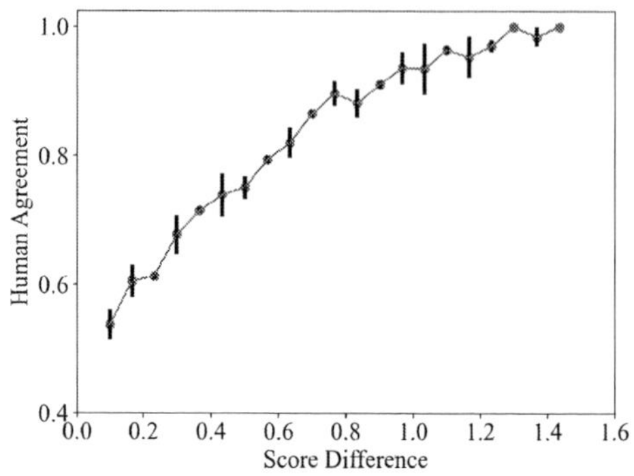

Figure 2: The figure shows the relationship between BWS score difference and human agreement. Blue dots with a blue connecting line represent the average human agreement a, and black bars represent their standard errors.

$$d = |S_a - S_b| \quad (1)$$

Then, let us consider N_c as the number of hierarchical pairs matching the hierarchical relationship derived from the BWS score, and N_w as the number of hierarchical pairs which contradict the hierarchical relationship derived from the BWS score (e.g., given a pair of memes A and B with BWS score of $b_A = 1$ and $b_B = -1$, and if we derived the three following hierarchical pairs $(A > B)$, $(A > B)$, $(A < B)$, then N_c and N_w would be $N_c = 2$ and $N_w = 1$). Human agreement a is defined and calculated as follows.

$$a = \frac{N_c}{N_c + N_w} \quad (2)$$

Finally, BWS score differences were binned with a unit of $\Delta d = 0.07$, and the average human agreement scores were calculated. The result is shown in Figure 2.

It was observed that for meme pairs with a BWS score of more than 1.0, the average of human agreement reached around 0.9, and for those with a BWS score of more than 1.4, the average of human agreement was close to 1.0.

Therefore, we conducted an additional refining process to eliminate examples with BWS scores between -0.5 and 0.5. This refined dataset can be considered to contain memes that are mostly not influenced by interpersonal differences in humor perception. The refined dataset includes 1,450 annotated memes.

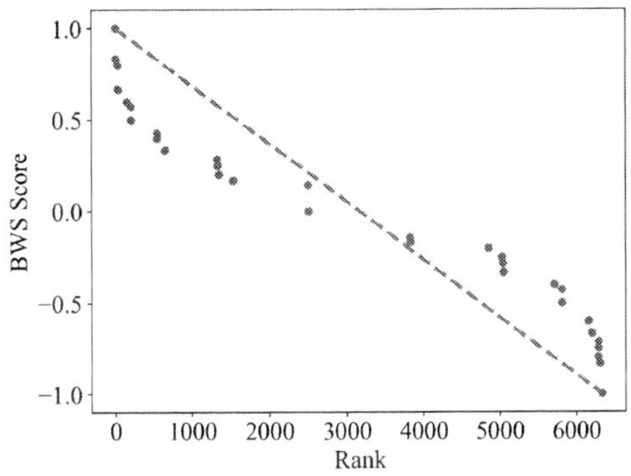

(a) Relationships between BWS score and ranks for the dataset before refinement.

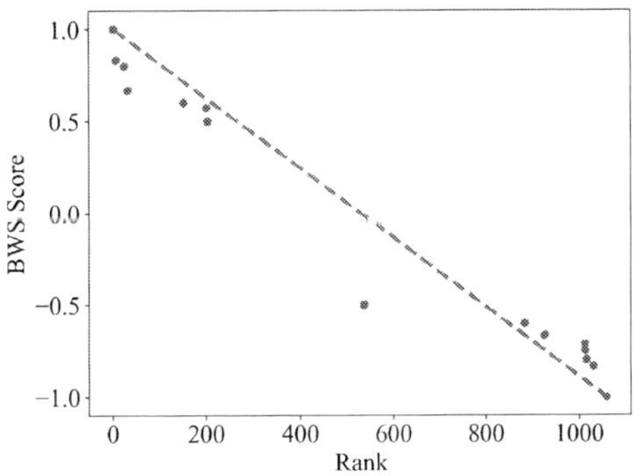

(b) Relationship between BWS score and rank for the refined dataset.

Figure 3: The figures show the relationship between BWS score and rank for the refined dataset. Blue dots represent examples of memes, and the red line indicates the hypothetical case of a uniform distribution of BWS scores.

3.5 Dataset Statistics

Figure 3 shows the relationship between BWS score and rankings of memes based on their BWS score for the dataset before and after refinement. It may be observed that before refinement, there were fewer examples with a BWS score close to 1 or -1 compared to those close to 0.

In terms of the refined dataset, there was a large gap between ranks 200 and 900. This means that examples with a BWS score of 0.5 or -0.5 constituted about half of the dataset, and examples with scores more than 0.5 or less than -0.5 were uniformly distributed.

In Figure 4, we provide two examples of memes from the refined dataset. These are examples of memes for which annotators were consistent regarding their degree of humor.

(a) An example of memes in the refined dataset with a BWS score of 1.

(b) An example of memes in the refined dataset that has a BWS score of -1.

Figure 4: This figure presents two examples of memes from the refined dataset. Annotators were consistent in their evaluation of the humor of these two memes.

To evaluate the consistency of the annotations in each dataset, we examined split-half reliability (SHR). SHR was calculated by first randomly splitting the annotation tasks into two halves. Thus, of the 3,801 tasks published on AMT, 1,900 tasks were designated as group A, and the other 1,901 tasks were designated as group B. Then, memes in each group were subjected to post-processing and the BWS scores of the memes were calculated separately. Finally, we analyzed Spearman's rank correlation coefficient between two rankings of memes based on the BWS scores calculated from groups A and B. As may be observed from Figure 5, the refinement process was able to eliminate examples that involved inconsistency in the perception of humor by annotators to improve the rank correlation coefficient.

3.6 Comparison with Other Meme Datasets

A comparison between our newly created dataset and some existing meme datasets is shown in Table 1. The ImgFlip575K Meme Dataset[5] compiles memes from the meme-generating website Imgflip[6]. While this dataset is exceptionally large, it does not include humor annotations by humans. The Memotion Dataset 7k was created for the sentiment analysis competition task in (Sharma et al., 2020). Although this dataset includes humor annotations created by human annotators, they were created using a rating scale, which is known to create biases in annotations (Kiritchenko and Mohammad, 2016). In comparison, our post-processed dataset is comparable to the Memotion dataset in size, while ensuring the reliability of annotations via the comparative annotation method and filtering post-

[5]https://github.com/schesa/ImgFlip575K_Dataset
[6]https://imgflip.com/

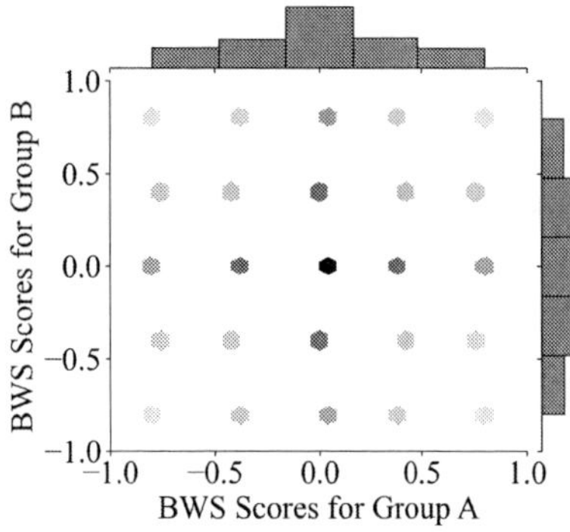

(a) Correlation between binned BWS scores for memes in group A and group B for the dataset before refinement.

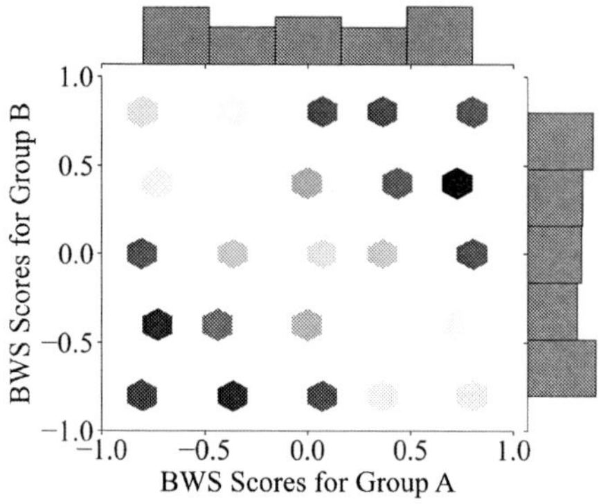

(b) Correlation between binned BWS scores for memes in groups A and B for the refined dataset.

Figure 5: The figures show the correlation between BWS scores for memes in groups A and B. To obtain this figure, BWS scores were binned in to 5 bins (-1 to -0.6, -0.6 to -0.2, -0.2 to 0.2, 0.2 to 0.6, 0.6 to 1). The darkness of each hexagon represents the number of memes plotted in each spot, with darker shades representing more memes. The Spearman's rank correlation coefficient for the post-processed dataset was 0.01, whereas that of the refined dataset was 0.52.

processing. Finally, to the best of our knowledge, our refined dataset is the only available dataset that considers interpersonal differences in the perception of humor and includes examples with consistent annotations.

4 Meme Evaluation Model Based on the Incongruity Theory

Studies have shown that many memes exhibit incongruities between images and their captions, which express humor (Yus, 2021). Therefore, we hypothesized that a module designed explicitly to extract incongruities between an image and its caption would improve a model's ability to classify whether a given meme is humorous.

To extract incongruities between image and text, we propose an incongruity extraction module consisting of CLIP image and text encoder (Radford et al., 2021), which is highlighted in orange in Figure 6. In this proposed method, a template image and caption are each fed into the corresponding pretrained CLIP encoder to obtain feature vectors of both the image ($\boldsymbol{v}_\mathrm{I} \in \mathbb{R}^{512}$) and the caption ($\boldsymbol{v}_\mathrm{T} \in \mathbb{R}^{512}$). Since pretrained CLIP encoders are trained such that the encoded feature vectors of a similar image and caption are located close to each other in the same latent space, we hypothesized that a feature vector $\boldsymbol{v}_\mathrm{CLIP} \in \mathbb{R}^{512}$ calculated by equation 3 would include encoded semantic information on the relativity of the input image to the input caption.

$$\boldsymbol{v}_\mathrm{CLIP} = \boldsymbol{v}_\mathrm{I} - \boldsymbol{v}_\mathrm{T} \tag{3}$$

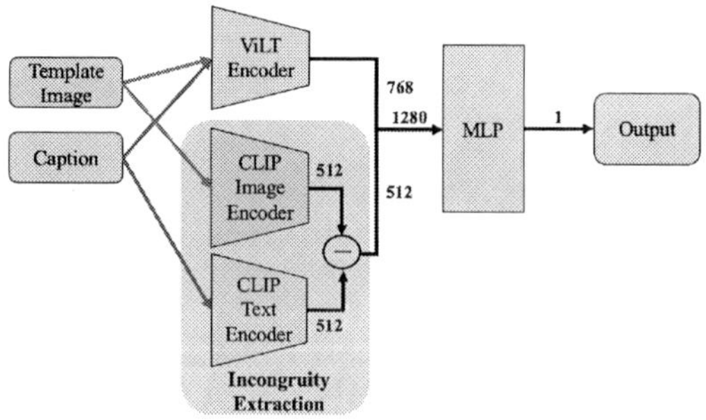

Figure 6: The figure shows an overview of the proposed method, which combines a module designed to extract incongruity between image and text with a ViLT encoder. In the incongruity extraction module, highlighted in orange, feature vectors of a template image and caption are extracted using the CLIP image and text encoders. The two resulting feature vectors are then subtracted and concatenated with the output of the ViLT encoder to be fed into an MLP. The numbers written next to the arrows represent the dimension of each vector.

We considered this information encoded in $\boldsymbol{v}_\mathrm{CLIP}$ to be useful in determining the level of incongruity between an image and its caption because image-text incongruity can be considered as a type of semantic relationship between image and text.

After obtaining $\boldsymbol{v}_\mathrm{CLIP}$ as a feature representing incongruity between an image and a caption, $\boldsymbol{v}_\mathrm{CLIP}$ is concatenated with the output features of a ViLT encoder ($\boldsymbol{v}_\mathrm{ViLT} \in \mathbb{R}^{768}$) and fed into a multilayer perceptron (MLP) model to predict whether a given meme is humorous, as shown in Figure 6.

Dataset	Instances	Humor Annotation by Human	Annotation Method	Ensured Reliability of Annotation	Ensured Consistency of Annotation
ImgFlip575K	575,948				
Memotion	6,991	✓	Rating-scale		
Raw (Ours)	7,500	✓	BWS		
Post-processed (Ours)	6,900	✓	BWS	✓	
Refined (Ours)	1,450	✓	BWS	✓	✓

Table 1: Comparison of our datasets to other meme datasets. Our post-processed dataset is comparable to the Memotion Dataset 7k in size, with the advantages of guaranteed reliability via BWS and the additional filtering processes. Our refined dataset ensures the consistency of the included humor annotations.

5 Experiments

5.1 Experimental Setting

To compare and evaluate the performance of the proposed method with the other models compared on the task of classifying humor in memes, we used 1,411 memes in the refined dataset with both upper and lower captions.

To train and evaluate the models, we conducted a ten-fold cross-validation, in which 1,411 memes were randomly divided into ten subsamples such that all memes with the same template image belonged to the same subsample. The memes were distributed such that all subsamples had approximately the same amount of memes. The subsample with a minimum number of memes had 131 memes, and that with a maximum number had 153.

To evaluate the models, each model was trained and evaluated ten times with the data divided into training, validation, and testing sets with a ratio of 8:1:1. For each evaluation step, the weight of the model that achieved the highest classification accuracy on the validation set was chosen to be evaluated on the testing set. We recorded classification accuracy scores calculated on ten different testing sets.

In addition, to minimize the effect of random initialization of the MLP model on the results of the evaluation, we conducted ten-fold cross validation with eight runs over different random seeds. Therefore, a total of 80 accuracy scores were obtained from each model, and the average accuracy score and standard error for each model were used for quantitative comparisons.

5.2 Models for Comparison

To validate the performance of the proposed model, we experimented with two additional models.

The first model encoded meme template images and captions into visual and textual features using a pretrained ViLT model (Kim et al., 2021b). As meme captions can be divided into upper and lower captions, a [SEP] token was inserted between these two parts before they were transformed into word embeddings. The output features of the ViLT encoder were then fed into an MLP model designed to output the probability with which a given meme could be classified as humorous.

In our proposed model, we supposed that the subtracted features of CLIP represented incongruity between an image and its caption, and considered this useful to improve performance on the humor classification task. To validate this statement, we implemented another model which did not subtract features provided by CLIP, but instead concatenated both encoded features of images and their captions to the ViLT output.

5.3 Parameters and Optimization Settings

All models in the experiment used three-layer MLPs with two hidden layers with a dimension of 768. A dropout layer with a dropout probability of 0.5 was added to all models to prevent overfitting. The models were trained with the objective of minimizing the binary cross-entropy loss using the Adam optimizer (Kingma and Ba, 2015). The weight decay parameter was set as 0.01, and the learning rate as 0.0001 for all models.

6 Results and Discussion

6.1 Quantitative Analysis

The result of the experiment is shown in Table 2. From the Table, it was observed that the proposed model (ViLT + CLIP incongruity) outperformed all other models for comparison. First, the proposed model was able to achieve around 5% better results compared to the model using only ViLT. This shows that the module designed to extract incongruities between image and text improved performance. Furthermore, the proposed model also outperformed the model that used ViLT and full

Model	Accuracy
ViLT	53.0 ± 0.2
ViLT+CLIP full feature	56.7 ± 0.4
ViLT+CLIP incongruity	**57.7 ± 0.4**

Table 2: The table show results of humor classification performance of the proposed model (ViLT + CLIP incongruity) and the other models compared.

CLIP features. This further strengthens our proposition that a model able to extract incongruities between image and text performs well in evaluating humor in memes, as the subtraction process of our proposed model extracted incongruities more explicitly compared to the baseline model using full CLIP features.

6.2 Qualitative Analysis

We also performed a qualitative analysis of the results to explore the characteristics of the proposed model. To conduct the analysis, we analyzed the classification results of the same testing set for all models used in the experiment.

We first recognized that both ViLT and the proposed model were able to identify memes with BWS scores greater than 0.7 as humorous with high accuracy. Out of ten memes with a BWS score greater than 0.7, ViLT was able to correctly identify nine as humorous, and the proposed model was able to correctly identify all ten. This signifies that memes that almost all annotators agreed were humorous were evaluated accurately by both ViLT and the proposed model.

In addition, the proposed model also outperformed other models in evaluating memes with BWS scores less than 0.7. Figure 7 shows two examples of memes that only the proposed model was able to correctly identify as humorous. The two memes involve incongruity between the image and the caption. The meme on the left is humorous because of the incongruity of an adult man making a childish statement about not wanting to do homework. In addition, the meme on the right also involves an incongruity between the image and the caption; it shows an intimidating man with a serious face, but the caption is pointing out a trivial notion, mocking people who post their every meal on social media.

In contrast, some examples of the analyzed memes showed a limitation of the proposed model; for some meme image templates, the proposed model seems to have output the classification based

(a) This meme is humorous because of the incongruity of an adult man making a childish statement about not wanting to do homework.

(b) This meme is humorous because of the incongruity between an intimidating man with a serious face and the trivial notion of mocking people who post their every meal on social media.

Figure 7: The figures show two examples of memes with image-caption incongruity, which only the proposed model was able to correctly identify as humorous.

only on the image. For example, for all memes created from a template image called "sad-trooper", the proposed model predicted the memes as not being humorous regardless of their captions. While we could not identify the cause of this limitation, it is possible that for some template images, the image feature vector obtained by CLIP was embedded in a space far from the embedded vectors of other meme image templates and captions. This would produce subtracted feature vectors that are almost the same for all memes with a given image template regardless of their captions.

7 Conclusion

Constructing a computational system to evaluate humor in memes is difficult due to the lack of datasets of memes with reliable and consistent humor annotations and the complexity of searching and extracting cross-modal incongruities between images and their captions. To overcome these challenges, we first created a dataset of memes annotated using BWS and proposed a refining process which was able to eliminate examples of memes affected by interpersonal differences in the perception of humor. Then, we used the refined dataset to train and validate the effectiveness of the proposed method, which was designed to extract incongruities between images and their captions to accurately classify whether a given meme is humorous. The experimental results showed that the proposed model was able to extract and utilize incongruities between images and their associated captions to outperform other multi-modal models on the humor classification task. This demonstrates the importance of using features that represent incongruities when evaluating humor in memes. Possible future work includes using the features representing incongruities not only to evaluate but also to generate new humorous memes from text or image input.

Acknowledgments

This work was partially supported by JST AIP Acceleration Research JPMJCR20U3, Moonshot R&D Grant Number JPMJPS2011, CREST Grant Number JPMJCR2015, JSPS KAKENHI Grant Number JP19H01115, and Basic Research Grant (Super AI) of Institute for AI and Beyond of the University of Tokyo. We would like to thank Hiromichi Kamata and Kohei Uehara for the helpful discussions. Furthermore, we would like to thank Yusuke Kurose and Miyuki Kajisa for their support in creating the dataset, and Editage (www.editage.com) for English language editing.

References

Issa Annamoradnejad and Gohar Zoghi. 2020. Colbert: Using bert sentence embedding for humor detection. *arXiv preprint arXiv:2004.12765*.

Hans Baumgartner and Jan-Benedict EM Steenkamp. 2001. Response styles in marketing research: A cross-national investigation. *Journal of marketing research*, 38(2):143–156.

Moniek Buijzen and Patti M Valkenburg. 2004. Developing a typology of humor in audiovisual media. *Media psychology*, 6(2):147–167.

Arjun Chandrasekaran, Ashwin K Vijayakumar, Stanislaw Antol, Mohit Bansal, Dhruv Batra, C Lawrence Zitnick, and Devi Parikh. 2016. We are humor beings: Understanding and predicting visual humor. In *The IEEE / CVF Computer Vision and Pattern Recognition Conference*.

Adam Finn and Jordan J Louviere. 1992. Determining the appropriate response to evidence of public concern: the case of food safety. *Journal of Public Policy & Marketing*, 11(2):12–25.

R Kelly Garrett and Shannon Poulsen. 2019. Flagging facebook falsehoods: Self-identified humor warnings outperform fact checker and peer warnings. *Journal of Computer-Mediated Communication*, 24(5):240–258.

Yingmei Guo, Jinfa Huang, Yanlong Dong, and Mingxing Xu. 2020. Guoym at SemEval-2020 task 8: Ensemble-based classification of visuo-lingual metaphor in memes. In *Proceedings of the Fourteenth Workshop on Semantic Evaluation*, pages 1120–1125, Barcelona (online). International Committee for Computational Linguistics.

Sojung Claire Kim, Emily K Vraga, and John Cook. 2021a. An eye tracking approach to understanding misinformation and correction strategies on social media: The mediating role of attention and credibility to reduce hpv vaccine misperceptions. *Health communication*, 36(13):1687–1696.

Wonjae Kim, Bokyung Son, and Ildoo Kim. 2021b. Vilt: Vision-and-language transformer without convolution or region supervision. In *International Conference on Machine Learning*, pages 5583–5594. The Proceedings of Machine Learning Research (PMLR).

Diederik P. Kingma and Jimmy Ba. 2015. Adam: A method for stochastic optimization. In *3rd International Conference on Learning Representations, ICLR 2015, San Diego, CA, USA, May 7-9, 2015, Conference Track Proceedings*.

Svetlana Kiritchenko and Saif Mohammad. 2017. Best-worst scaling more reliable than rating scales: A case study on sentiment intensity annotation. In *Annual Meeting of the Association for Computational Linguistics (ACL)*.

Svetlana Kiritchenko and Saif M. Mohammad. 2016. Capturing reliable fine-grained sentiment associations by crowdsourcing and best–worst scaling. In *Proceedings of The 15th Annual Conference of the North American Chapter of the Association for Computational Linguistics: Human Language Technologies (NAACL)*, San Diego, California.

Jordan J. Louviere. 1992. Experimental choice analysis: Introduction and overview. *Journal of Business Research*, 24(2):89–95.

Paul E. McGhee. 1989. Chapter 5: The contribution of humor to children's social development. *Journal of Children in Contemporary Society*, 20(1-2):119–134.

Saša Petrović and David Matthews. 2013. Unsupervised joke generation from big data. In *Proceedings of the 51st Annual Meeting of the Association for Computational Linguistics (Volume 2: Short Papers)*, pages 228–232, Sofia, Bulgaria. Association for Computational Linguistics.

Barbara Plester. 2009. Healthy humour: Using humour to cope at work. *Kotuitui: New Zealand Journal of Social Sciences Online*, 4:89–102.

Alec Radford, Jong Wook Kim, Chris Hallacy, Aditya Ramesh, Gabriel Goh, Sandhini Agarwal, Girish Sastry, Amanda Askell, Pamela Mishkin, Jack Clark, et al. 2021. Learning transferable visual models from natural language supervision. In *International Conference on Machine Learning*, pages 8748–8763. The Proceedings of Machine Learning Research (PMLR).

Victor Raskin. 1985. *Semantic mechanisms of humor*. D. Reidel.

Julia Rayz. 2004. Computationally recognizing word-play in jokes. *Cognitive Science - COGSCI.*

Willibald Ruch and Franz-Josef Hehl. 2010. A two-mode model of humor appreciation: Its relation to aesthetic appreciation and simplicity-complexity of personality. In *The sense of humor*, pages 109–142. De Gruyter Mouton.

Howard Schuman and Stanley Presser. 1996. *Questions and answers in attitude surveys: Experiments on question form, wording, and context.* Sage.

Chhavi Sharma, Deepesh Bhageria, William Paka, Scott, Srinivas P Y K L, Amitava Das, Tanmoy Chakraborty, Viswanath Pulabaigari, and Björn Gambäck. 2020. SemEval-2020 Task 8: Memotion Analysis-The Visuo-Lingual Metaphor! In *Proceedings of the 14th International Workshop on Semantic Evaluation (SemEval-2020)*, Barcelona, Spain. Association for Computational Linguistics.

Emily K Vraga, Sojung Claire Kim, and John Cook. 2019. Testing logic-based and humor-based corrections for science, health, and political misinformation on social media. *Journal of Broadcasting & Electronic Media*, 63(3):393–414.

Hiroaki Yamane, Yusuke Mori, and Tatsuya Harada. 2021. Humor meets morality: Joke generation based on moral judgement. *Information Processing & Management*, 58(3):102520.

Sara K. Yeo and Meaghan McKasy. 2021. Emotion and humor as misinformation antidotes. In *Proceedings of the National Academy of Sciences of the United States of America(PNAS).*

Tomohiro Yoshikawa and Ryosuke Iwakura. 2020. Study on development of humor discriminator for dialogue system. *Journal of Advanced Computational Intelligence and Intelligent Informatics*, 24(3):422–435.

Francisco Yus. 2021. Incongruity-resolution humorous strategies in image macro memes. *Internet Pragmatics*, pages 131–149.

Yftah Ziser, Elad Kravi, and David Carmel. 2020. Humor detection in product question answering systems. In *Proceedings of the 43rd International ACM SIGIR Conference on Research and Development in Information Retrieval*, page 519–528. Association for Computing Machinery.

A Appendix

A.1 AMT Interface for Annotating Humor in Memes

In this section, we provide examples of the interface shown to annotators of AMT to obtain humor annotations of memes.

In Section 1 (questions 1 - 24), annotators were first asked to select one of three choices on their understanding of the meme provided, as shown in Figure 8. Memes identified as not in English were eliminated in the post-process.

Then, annotators were asked to write up to three words in the caption that were necessary to understand the meme, as shown in Figure 9. If the presented meme was not in English, the annotators were asked to input "NIE" in the first box and leave the other two boxes blank. It was designed such that if an annotator entered a word that is not in the meme presented, the interface would show an error saying, "You may not input a word that is not in the caption".

The two questions shown in Figure 8 and 9 were asked for 12 separate memes within a task, constituting the first 24 questions presented to the annotators.

Finally, in Section 2 (questions 25 - 27), annotators were asked to choose the most and least humorous meme from among the four presented, as shown in Figure 10. It was ensured that annotators could not select the same meme as most and least humorous. Memes presented in questions 25 - 27 are identical to the memes that were annotated in questions 1 - 24.

Question 11

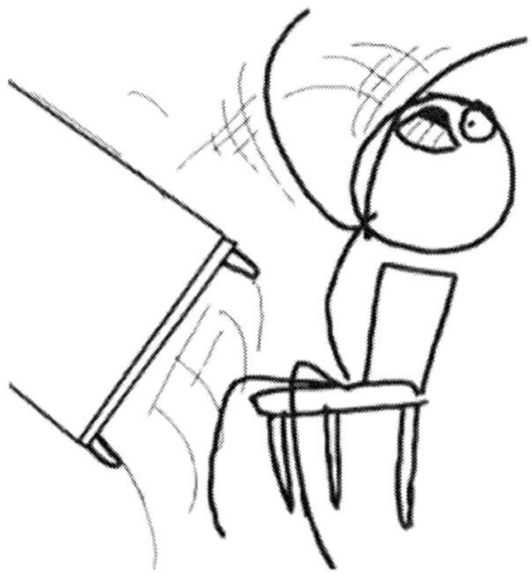

actually does homework..

doesnt get checked

Do you understand the humor in this meme?

○ **1** Yes, I understand the humor.

○ **2** No, I do not understand the humor although it is in English.

○ **3** This meme is not in English.

Figure 8: AMT interface asking annotators to select their understanding of the meme. Annotators were asked to choose whether they understood the humor in the meme or if the meme was not in English. This question was used to filter-out memes that were not in English. This question was asked for 12 separate memes in each task.

Question 12

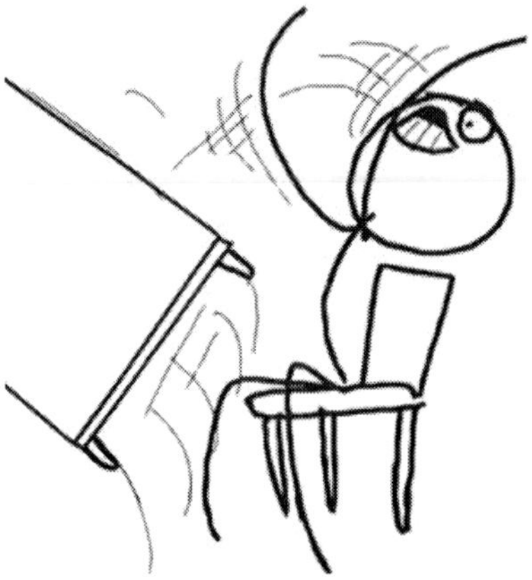

actually does homework..

doesnt get checked

Please **write 1 ~ 3 words in the caption** that you think are necessary to understand the humor in the following boxs. If the meme is **not** in English, **write "NIE" in the first box** and leave other boxes blank. Please be aware that writing "NIE" for captions that **are in English** can lead to **rejection** of your work.

Word 1 (* required):

Word 2:

Word 3:

Figure 9: AMT interface asking annotators to write up to three words that are necessary to understand the meme. This question was used to extract important words to understand the humor in memes (humor anchor).

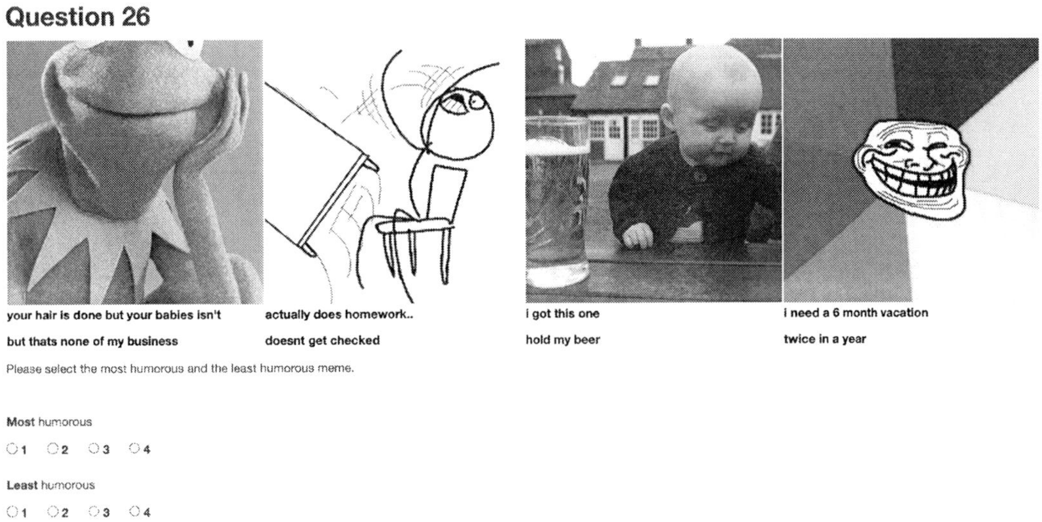

Figure 10: AMT interface asking annotators to choose the most and least humorous meme out of the four presented. The annotations were used to calculate the BWS score of each meme.

Author Index

Association for Computational Linguistics
209 N. Eighth Street
Stroudsburg, Pennsylvania 18360

ISBN 978-1-7138-6146-1

CURRAN ASSOCIATES INC.
proceedings.com